Robertson Davies
(1913–1995)

Nicholas Maes

Nicholas Maes teaches classics at the University of Waterloo and is also a high school history teacher in Toronto. His adult novel *Dead Man's Float* (Véhicule) was published in 2006, and he has published several short stories and reviews in a variety of journals, including *The Fiddlehead*, *Books in Canada*, and *The Dalhousie Review*. Recently, for Dundurn Press, he published *Locksmith*, his first novel for young people. Originally from Montreal, he now lives in Toronto with his wife, three children, and a rabbit.

In the same collection

Ven Begamudré, *Isaac Brock: Larger Than Life*
Lynne Bowen, *Robert Dunsmuir: Laird of the Mines*
Kate Braid, *Emily Carr: Rebel Artist*
Kathryn Bridge, *Phyllis Munday: Mountaineer*
William Chalmers, *George Mercer Dawson: Geologist, Scientist, Explorer*
Anne Cimon, *Susanna Moodie: Pioneer Author*
Deborah Cowley, *Lucille Teasdale: Doctor of Courage*
Gary Evans, *John Grierson: Trailblazer of Documentary Film*
Judith Fitzgerald, *Marshall McLuhan: Wise Guy*
lian goodall, *William Lyon Mackenzie King: Dreams and Shadows*
Tom Henighan, *Vilhjalmur Stefansson: Arctic Adventurer*
Stephen Eaton Hume, *Frederick Banting: Hero, Healer, Artist*
Naïm Kattan, *A.M. Klein: Poet and Prophet*
Betty Keller, *Pauline Johnson: First Aboriginal Voice of Canada*
Heather Kirk, *Mazo de la Roche: Rich and Famous Writer*
Vladimir Konieczny, *Glenn Gould: A Musical Force*
Michelle Labrèche-Larouche, *Emma Albani: International Star*
Wayne Larsen, *A.Y. Jackson: A Love for the Land*
Wayne Larsen, *James Wilson Morrice: Painter of Light and Shadow*
Francine Legaré, *Samuel de Champlain: Father of New France*
Margaret Macpherson, *Nellie McClung: Voice for the Voiceless*
Dave Margoshes, *Tommy Douglas: Building the New Society*
Marguerite Paulin, *René Lévesque: Charismatic Leader*
Marguerite Paulin, *Maurice Duplessis: Powerbroker, Politician*
Raymond Plante, *Jacques Plante: Behind the Mask*
T.F. Rigelhof, *George Grant: Redefining Canada*
Tom Shardlow, *David Thompson: A Trail by Stars*
Arthur Slade, *John Diefenbaker: An Appointment with Destiny*
Roderick Stewart, *Wilfrid Laurier: A Pledge for Canada*
Sharon Stewart, *Louis Riel: Firebrand*
André Vanasse, *Gabrielle Roy: A Passion for Writing*
John Wilson, *John Franklin: Traveller on Undiscovered Seas*
John Wilson, *Norman Bethune: A Life of Passionate Conviction*
Rachel Wyatt, *Agnes Macphail: Champion of the Underdog*

DAVIES

Robertson

MAGICIAN OF WORDS

DUNDURN PRESS
TORONTO

Project Editor: Michael Carroll
Editor: Barry Jowett
Copy Editor: Allison Hirst
Index: Darcy Dunton
Design: Jennifer Scott
Printer: Marquis

Cover and frontispiece: Davies in 1948. At the time he was the editor of the *Peterborough Examiner.*

Library and Archives Canada Cataloguing in Publication

Maes, Nicholas, 1960-
    Robertson Davies : magician of words / by Nicholas Maes.

Includes index.
ISBN 978-1-55002-872-0

    1. Davies, Robertson, 1913-1995. 2. Authors, Canadian (English)--20th century--Biography. I. Title.

PS8507.A67Z722 2009   C813'.54   C2008-906218-3

1 2 3 4 5   13 12 11 10 09

 Conseil des Arts du Canada   Canada Council for the Arts    ONTARIO ARTS COUNCIL CONSEIL DES ARTS DE L'ONTARIO

Canada

We acknowledge the support of the **Canada Council for the Arts** and the **Ontario Arts Council** for our publishing program. We also acknowledge the financial support of the **Government of Canada** through the **Book Publishing Industry Development Program** and **The Association for the Export of Canadian Books**, and the **Government of Ontario** through the **Ontario Book Publishers Tax Credit program**, and the **Ontario Media Development Corporation**.

Printed and bound in Canada.
Printed on recycled paper.

www.dundurn.com

Dundurn Press
3 Church Street, Suite 500
Toronto, Ontario, Canada
M5E 1M2

Gazelle Book Services Limited
White Cross Mills
High Town, Lancaster, England
LA1 4XS

Dundurn Press
2250 Military Road
Tonawanda, NY
U.S.A. 14150

Contents

Author's Note

While the events of Robertson Davies's life have been described as factually as possible, the conversations presented in this book together with the letter from Eleanor Sweezey have been reconstructed from secondary source material.

The Thamesfield Herald *office. Rupert Davies is at the back, operating the platen press, Fred is at the stone in the middle, and Arthur is reading a paper (front).*

Prologue

On a hot summer day, when he was six years old, Robertson Davies was playing in the attic of the family home in Renfrew, Ontario — a red-brick, two-storey house with indoor plumbing (a rarity at the time). He was pretending to work a newspaper press, like his father Rupert, when he heard a faint scratching from behind. At first he ignored it, thinking it was a bird that had alighted on an eave outside, but when it persisted he finally looked around in annoyance.

He frowned slightly. A few feet ahead of him stood a low, wooden closet, and the persistent scratching was coming from inside. It had to be a mouse or squirrel. How fortunate the closet door was closed. When he went downstairs he would tell his mother about this pest and they would lay some traps and …

His blood froze. The light in the room was somehow brighter, yet had a blood-red tinge to its edges. The room's temperature was noticeably cooler and he felt he was not in the house any longer but was a million miles away from his mother and ... safety. And that was strange. Although the closet door was still decidedly in place, a glow was suddenly coming from inside it and ... How weird! He could see inside! And what was that?... A figure of some sort was taking shape ...

He almost screamed. An ancient woman was staring out at him, gnarled and misshapen and with a look of pure malevolence. She smiled slowly, her few teeth yellow and disfigured with decay. He could not move. He could not blink. His lungs refused to take in breath.

For what seemed like half an hour — although it might have been a matter of seconds — the pair of them continued to stare at each other, the witch never altering her malignant expression. Then, without warning, just as Davies thought she was going to blast him with a spell, she disappeared. One moment she was there; the next she was gone.

Davies felt himself to check his bones were intact then glanced furtively around the room. The light was back to normal now and warm to the touch. His mother's voice was drifting up from the kitchen — she was warbling Tosti's "Goodbye." And the closet was just a closet now, with nothing but a few trunks containing old clothes. He sighed with relief and made his way to the steps.

Even as he ran downstairs, however, he knew this visitation had been real and things, normal things, were not what they seemed.

1

Childhood

What really shapes and conditions and makes us is somebody only a few of us ever have the courage to face: and that is the child you once were, long before formal education ever got its claws into you — that impatient, all demanding child who wants love and power and can't get enough of either and who goes on raging and weeping in your spirit till at last your eyes are closed and all the fools say, "Doesn't he look peaceful?" It is those pent-up, craving children who make all the wars and all the horrors and all the art and all the beauty and discovery in life, because they are trying to achieve what lay beyond their grasp before they were five years old.

(*The Rebel Angels*)

Robertson Davies at the age of one.

> It's a wise child that knows his father, but it's
> one child in a million who knows his mother.
> They're a mysterious mob, mothers.
> (*What's Bred in the Bone*)

Aware that yet another life of William Robertson Davies is being written, the Lesser Zadkiel and the Daemon Maimas have decided to meet. As the Angel of Biography, Zadkiel wishes to question Maimas, who served as Davies's guardian spirit while the writer was alive.

"So we meet again, Maimas. Has long has it been?"

"That's an easy one, Zadkiel. We last congregated when my old charge, Robertson, was working on his novel *What's Bred in the Bone* in the early 1980s and happened to invoke us."

"Did he know at the time that we truly existed? More important, did he have any inkling that, the same way you were Francis Cornish's protective daemon, so too were you his guardian and source of inspiration?"

"You could never tell with Robertson. For all his book-learning, theatricality, and crusty mannerisms, he was deeply attuned to the supernatural. That was partly my doing, you know. I made sure that at an early age he'd be sensitive to realities beyond the humdrum facts."

"That's what I want to ask you about. Davies has always puzzled me. He belonged to that generation that witnessed so many changes, and on top of that his father was a journalist and all over the news, as he himself was for over twenty years. And yet he often ignored the events around him and fixed his eyes on ... something else."

"Yes. Quite right, Zadkiel. Unlike most people his age, Davies experienced a journey that was internal more than anything else. I decided early on in the game that he would be primarily a novelist by occupation — a chronicler of the human spirit and its fascinating peregrinations. There is a pattern to his life. In other words ...

"Be a good fellow and point it out to me, Maimas."

"Nothing would give me greater pleasure, Zadkiel."

Robertson Davies would become known as one of Canada's most daring and imaginative writers — a strong proponent of feeling and artistic accomplishment over reason and bland common sense. It is greatly ironic, therefore, that at the very start of his story — his family's origins — characters appear who do not seem the type to produce a cast of mind as whimsical as Davies's. His ancestors, his parents included, while interested in literature and art, were hard-headed, practical people who were first and foremost concerned with earning a living and placed little stock in artistic achievement. And who could blame them? Their circumstances had been very hard, and romantic notions about the artist's "inner journey" would have compromised their ability to survive.

On his mother Florence's side, Davies was the descendant of English, Dutch, and Scottish pioneers. In the late eighteenth century her English ancestors had retreated to Canada along with other United Empire Loyalists when the American colonies were battling the English throne. One relative in particular, Mary Jones Gage, had lost her husband to the fighting and canoed with her two children to the western half of the province of Quebec (to be known one year later as Upper Canada) where she bought herself a farm near the city of Hamilton. Some years later the famous battle of Stoney Creek was fought on her property during the War of 1812.

Florence's Scottish forebears had been deprived of their land in the Scottish Highlands and been sold to the British, who had transported them to the James Bay region. This area had been isolated, infertile, and bone-numbingly cold and, desperate to escape it, they made their way by foot to the southern part of modern-day Ontario, enduring incalculable hardships en route. Understandably, the relations on this side

Rupert Davies, Robertson Davies's father, taken about 1900.

Davies's mother, Florence McKay, in 1898.

of the family had been pragmatic, joyless, and hostile to the arts, and had passed this sour attitude down to their children and their children's children. Florence's own father had been a particularly explosive character: addicted to morphine, which he had initially taken for his asthma, he suffered furious temper tantrums during which he occasionally chased his wife with a carving knife in hand.

Davies's father, Rupert, was similarly marked by his background. His family had owned a modest tailor business in Welshpool, Wales. Despite Spartan living conditions — the family of seven lived in quarters above the store — Rupert's childhood had been comfortable enough. In the early 1890s, however, an agricultural depression affected business. Rupert's father, Walter, could no longer provide for all five children and encouraged the fifteen-year-old Rupert and his older brother Percy to immigrate to Canada in 1894. As a young, vulnerable immigrant, Rupert happily accepted work in a stable. Greatly taken with the newspaper business, in which he had no experience, he embarked on an apprenticeship at the age of seventeen as a junior printer in Brantford, Ontario.

After passing difficult exams for the Typographical Union in 1900, he worked in Toronto and New York as a printer, but returned to Brantford because he missed his family. He then fell in love with Florence McKay, admiring her no-nonsense attitude, and married her on October 16, 1901, despite her family's apprehensions that he would never amount to much. Over the next few years he fathered two sons and worked as a typesetter and journalist until, in 1908, he purchased the *Thamesville Herald*. The acquisition of this paper marked the start of his career as a publisher, and in subsequent decades he would earn himself a tidy fortune, procure himself an estate in

Wales, and, in 1947, become a member of the Canadian Senate. Although raw talent and native intelligence carried him forward, his hard-headedness and willingness to work impossible hours were primarily responsible for his noteworthy success. While very fond of theatre and the arts, and imbued with the Welsh facility for language, he was decidedly more a businessman than he was a literary craftsman.

Towards the end of his life Davies would write about his relatives in his novel *Murther and Walking Spirits*. In this book, the ghost of murdered Connor Gilmartin watches a series of films that chronicle in detail the lives of his (and Davies's) ancestors. At the end of the proceedings, Connor comments to himself:

> My festival has taken me into the past, though not really very far into the past, of my own fore-bears. Taken me into the eighteenth century, which is no distance in the procession of human history, but far enough to tell me more about the American strand and the Old Country strand which, in me, were woven into what is now indisputably a Canadian weftage. Given substance to people, many of whom were strangers to me, or at best names to which no special character attached, but whose courage and resource, loyalty even to the point of self-destruction, crankiness and meanness, despair and endurance are now known to me, and arouse my admiration, my pity and — I must say it, strange as it seems to me — my love.

And then William Robertson Davies stumbled onto the scene — he was named after Rupert's younger brother, who had died two years before from tuberculosis. Born August 28, 1913, Davies appeared in the world when his father's fortunes were starting to take off. The *Thamesville Herald* earned Rupert a reasonable living, and its sale in 1919 would provide him with a handsome profit, which he would reinvest in other papers. Unlike his brothers Fred and Arthur, who were, respectively, eleven and ten years older than he, Davies never experienced the years when Rupert had toiled to the point of nervous exhaustion and received paltry compensation for his efforts. Instead, he grew up in spacious houses with electricity, plumbing, and conveniences.

His early childhood, too, coincided with a period when Canadians as a whole lived in comparatively rough circumstances. In the year of his birth, Canada was merely forty-six years old, Saskatchewan and Alberta had been Canadian provinces for only eight years, Manitoba had only reached its present geographical size the year before, and Newfoundland and Labrador would not join Confederation for another thirty-six years. The Canadian population stood at roughly seven million souls, over a million of whom had arrived as immigrants between 1911 and 1913, with not much more than the shirts on their backs.

Canada was still very much influenced by Great Britain: its foreign policy, under the British North America Act, was wholly controlled by the English Parliament in London. Great Britain itself, and not the United States, was at this time the world's greatest superpower: it controlled some twenty-five percent of the world's total land mass and ruled about a quarter of the global population. The world, too, was in some sense larger: travel by air was still in its infancy — it would be another fourteen years before Charles Lindbergh crossed the Atlantic in his *Spirit of St.*

Louis — and the journey to Europe from Montreal or New York City would take a traveller at least seven days.

While electricity and running water were becoming a little more common in people's dwellings, only the wealthy could afford such labour-saving devices as the sewing and washing machine, the vacuum cleaner, and the refrigerator. Large numbers of Canadians were toiling as farmers, lumberjacks, fishermen, and (generally speaking) hewers of wood and drawers of water. With the introduction of the Ford Model T five years earlier, cars were affordable and becoming more of an everyday sight, but they had by no means yet supplanted the horse and buggy, even in the large metropolitan centres.

Thamesville, Davies's place of birth, was hardly a metropolitan centre. It was a quiet, prosperous farming village in southwest Ontario where, to the extent that Davies could remember his earliest years, his experiences were positive. Thamesville would later serve as the basis for Deptford in Davies's *Fifth Business*, and here is his evaluation of the town that he presents in that novel:

> Once it was the fashion to represent villages as places inhabited by laughable, lovable simpletons, unspotted by the worldliness of city life, though occasionally shrewd in rural concerns. Later it was the popular thing to show villages as rotten with vice ... while a rigid piety was professed in the streets. Our village never seemed to me to be like that. It was more varied in what it offered to the observer than people from bigger and more sophisticated places generally think, and if it had sins and follies and roughnesses,

it also had much to show of virtue, dignity, and
even of nobility.

It was in this modest town that Davies attended the Presbyterian Church, listened to records on his parents' Victrola, and
frequently visited his father at work, admiring the paper's type-
setting machine and platen press. He was read to from an early
age: his parents were adamant in exposing him to the Bible, fairy
tales, and various children's classics, while his brother introduced
him to the funny papers. And because every family member was
part of his father's newspaper business, to the point that each was
expected to write the occasional column, it was assumed Davies
would be a writer, too. From the moment he learned to speak, his
parents not only insisted on the right enunciation of words, but
corrected his grammar at every turn. They even kept a dictionary
near the dinner table to verify the usage of words that popped up
in conversation or to authenticate their proper spelling.

The one routine in his early childhood that Davies resented
was a loathsome, weekly treatment — one in keeping with
medical ideas of the time: Dr. Tyrrell's Domestic Internal Bath.
This was a large rubber cushion with a nozzle in its centre. Once
its interior had been filled with warm water, the "patient" would
be positioned in such a way that the nozzle would penetrate his
rear and his weight against the cushion would cause the water to
shoot into his bowels. Purgation would swiftly follow. Although
such exercises were considered normal, indeed healthy, Davies
would later opine, through his character David Staunton in his
novel *The Manticore*, how such medical therapies amounted to
"the wildest nonsense and cruelty."

One would never guess from the tranquility of Davies's early
years that a war was raging over in Europe — the War to End

All Wars. For most of Davies's early childhood, Canadians were scraping their resources together to fight for King and Country overseas in France and Flanders. Because trench warfare (the standard form of combat in this war) required an enormous investment of manpower, over a period of four years Canada shipped some 600,000 troops abroad, of whom some 65,000 lost their lives in battle through wounds, infection, or bad living conditions. Ypres, the Somme, Passchendaele, and Vimy Ridge were roiling, violent battlefields where Canadian troops more than proved their mettle but paid a heavy price in doing so. To keep this huge army equipped and fed, Canadians back home had to tighten their belts and labour hard in the fields and the country's manufacturing plants. In the absence of so many males, women filled positions that before the war had been off limits to them. While this period would pave the way for future progress and prosperity, it was a fiercely difficult time that left deep scars on the population.

It was in 1919, one year after the war had ended, that Rupert moved his family to Renfrew, Ontario, after selling off the *Thamesville Herald* and acquiring a new paper, the *Renfrew Mercury*. This new locale was not to Davies's liking. Whereas Thamesville was located in rich, open farmland, the larger Renfrew, sixty miles northwest of Ottawa, was primarily a logging town and accessible only by rail. The local population was suspicious of outsiders and, from Davies's perspective, was ungenerous and cruel: one memory of his was how the townsfolk teased a dwarf so remorselessly that they finally drove this character to take his own life. But it was his experience at Renfrew's North Ward elementary school that went furthest in colouring his impression of his townsmen.

"Hey Davies! Why yuh wearin' those sissy jackets? Yuh like

dressin' like a girl?" one particularly rough boy would insult him daily in the schoolyard.

"At least my parents don't sew me into my underwear in winter."

"Yuh stuck-up pig! Yuh think yuh's better than me?"

"I certainly couldn't be worse."

"Yeah? D'yuh know what I'm goin' to tell yuh? I pass yer house at night and there's a light on in a room at the top. Yuh know why? 'Cause a lunatic relative lives there and yuh doesn't even know it! Yuh got lunatic blood in yuhs!"

In addition to his tormentors in Renfrew's streets, Davies had to endure a trying climate at home. Despite their many common interests, Rupert and Florence had gradually become estranged from each other. Rupert discovered, several years into the couple's marriage, that his wife had deceived him about her age: instead of being five years his senior, she was in fact nine years older than him. Over time, he came to greatly resent what appeared to be an act of duplicity on her part. And because his newspaper holdings expanded at this stage and provided him with a taste of genuine wealth, he began to delight in socializing with others and exploring the world beyond his small-town boundaries. Florence, for her part, remained at home and, very often, was bedridden with illness.

Davies would later offer an additional explanation for his parents' alienation from each other in his novel *The Cunning Man* (1994). Modelling his character "Brocky" Gilmartin's parents on his own, he would have Brocky say the following of them, after his friend Jonathan Hullah has taken note of the disaffection between them:

> My mother, you see, is a real New World person.
> Old Loyalist stock, left the States at the time of

the Revolution. Great uncles killed defending Canada against the Yanks in 1812 — the whole thing. She simply hasn't any attachment to the Old World at all. What she knows of it, she mistrusts. But my father — he's lived most of his life in this country, and he's done some quite good things for the country as well as for himself — but there's a part of him that's never left Wales. *Hen Wlad fy'Nhadau* — old Land of my Fathers — it's bred in the bone with him, you see, and she's jealous of it. Funny isn't it, for a woman to be jealous not of another woman who has a hold on her husband, but of a country. But that's it. She wants to possess him utterly, and she wants to possess me, and he won't have it.

These household tensions affected Davies's relations with his mother. At this time, because childbirth claimed many women's lives, children were encouraged to believe that they had come into the world at great risk to their mothers. In consequence they were expected to pay full respect to their mothers and show them absolute obedience. Davies found this difficult. Perhaps Florence's advanced age made her impatient with her youngest (she was forty-three when she gave birth to Davies); perhaps the friction between her husband and her pushed her nerves to their very limit; perhaps she clung too tenaciously to her youngest, fearing abandonment by her family as Rupert pursued his interests and her older sons entered adulthood; perhaps Davies himself had an excessively strong personality. One way or another, their exchanges could be trying.

"You forgot to light the oven! Your father's supper won't be ready when he comes home!"

"It might help in future if you left me a note."

"How dare you! I'm your mother! I'm not some schoolyard tough whom you can sauce as you please!"

"Not the pony whip!"

"Come here!"

"I won't! You're going to whip me!"

When Rupert intervened in these disputes, he invariably stuck up for his wife, and would remind Davies that he owed his life to his mother and that he should love her without question or doubt. These arguments always ended the same way.

"Bow down, Bobbie."

"Do I have to?"

"Yes. Now beg your mother's forgiveness for your monstrous show of insolence. Go on!"

"Please forgive me, Mother."

"And swear you'll love her always."

"I swear I will always love you, Mother."

"Now seal your promise by kissing her left shoe."

A further source of humiliation was Davies's struggle in arithmetic. Whereas he was a first-rate student in other subjects, and was reading books that were well beyond the reach of his peers, he was hopeless with anything having to do with numbers. This disability would come to haunt him in later years and prove inconvenient.

And then there were the frequent visitations by that witch. Sometimes she, or a similar spectre, would appear at the foot of his bed, fixing him always with that murderous stare. Davies's powers of visualization were so strong that he did not think of these as dreams so much as visions with a basis in reality. Because recourse to his parents was out of the question, these apparitions made him miserable.

"Leave me alone!" he whispered fiercely to the shadowy crone as she crouched at the start of his bed yet again and stared at him with murder in her eyes. "What do you want from me? Why can't you bother Fred or Arthur?"

This is not to say that Davies's years in Renfrew were utterly intolerable. He eventually learned to defend himself at school and, a piece of rare fortune, was transferred in third grade to an institute that was more to his liking. He attended the movies regularly, greatly enjoying the screen antics of Buster Keaton, Charlie Chaplin, and other silent greats, and was taken to numerous concerts and the occasional opera in Toronto and at the Chautauqua music festival. The circus often came to Renfrew, too, and here he visited a variety of sideshows, whose bearded ladies and contortionists strongly appealed to his imagination. These memories would serve him well in later years when he set about writing his novel *World of Wonders*. It was in this period, too, that he developed several passions that he would pursue the length of his days.

At the age of nine he published his first newspaper article, a story about a minister's lecture on Shakespeare that appeared on the front page of the *Renfrew Mercury*. Although the piece was very well-constructed for a nine-year-old, he thought little of this accomplishment because he was surrounded by a household of journalists. The article was merely the first of several thousand that he would pen through the course of a long writing career.

He also became an avid reader. The first story he managed to read on his own was a big disappointment, *The Little Red Hen*. The tale involves a hen that asks the cat, the dog, and the pig to help her prepare a loaf of bread. After they refuse, leaving her to toil on her own, she denies them a share of the bread, on the grounds that they have done nothing to earn it. Interestingly enough, Davies detested this story. The hen did not know that the dog had guarded the barnyard, that the pig had enlightened them with his philosophy and dignified bearing, and that the cat had amused them all with her singing and beauty. At the heart of Davies's reaction to this tale was his awareness that the true artist contributes as much to society as anyone else.

Happily, his disgust with his first taste of reading did not colour his general taste for books. Before long he was plowing his way through boys' almanacs and the various English classics: *The Swiss Family Robinson*, *Little Men* and *Little Women*, *Robinson Crusoe*, as well as more complicated novels by Dickens, Mary Shelley, and Thomas Hardy. The latter's *Tess of the d'Urbervilles* proved a little too sophisticated for his child's mind, but he read it through to the end anyway. It was at this stage in his boyhood that he began laying the foundations of his encyclopedic knowledge of Western literature and the English canon.

Renfrew possessed a single theatre and, although its stage productions were rather shoddy affairs, Davies had the opportunity to absorb a number of plays at an early age: Augustin McHugh's *Officer 666*, Gilbert and Sullivan's *H.M.S. Pinafore*, Brandon Thomas's massively popular *Charley's Aunt*, and the stage version of *Uncle Tom's Cabin*. Davies had not yet developed the theatre "bug," but he did study the staging closely and was delighted when he pieced together how certain effects had been orchestrated.

His horizons expanded broadly, too, when he travelled to England at the age of eleven. As president of the Canadian Weekly Newspapers Association, his father decided in the summer of 1924 to lead a group of Canadian editors to Europe and to acquaint them with their English associates. Florence accompanied him, and Davies was invited to tag along.

For the space of five weeks Davies toured the British Isles, witnessing for himself a host of famous landmarks and experiencing the best that English civilization had to offer. He learned from first-hand experience that, alongside the fruits of English museums and theatre, Canada at that stage was culturally impoverished. At the same time he was able to visit various First World War battlefields in France, the scene of horrible carnage a mere six years earlier. He took careful mental notes, unaware that these memories would serve him well some forty years later when he composed his masterpiece *Fifth Business*. Overall, the British Isles and continental Europe would continue to lure him through the course of his life. Indeed, in 1932 his father would purchase an estate in Wales, and the Davies family would have a property to visit abroad.

Back in Canada another passion beckoned. In 1925 the American magician Harry Blackstone visited Renfrew. Famous for his ability to levitate a woman on a couch and cause her to vanish into thin air, the Great Blackstone had a powerful effect on Davies and triggered his lifelong interest in magic. He sent away for magic manuals and equipment advertised on the back page of comics. Despite his interest and lengthy hours of practice, however, his hands were clumsy and he proved a third-rate conjuror.

"Fred! Arthur! Watch this!"

"Not another trick, Bobbie! Don't you remember what happened last time?"

"Shh. I have to concentrate. Now, I want you to keep an eye on this egg ..."

"Is that a real egg or one you're about to lay?"

"Pay attention! I'm going to make it vanish ... Abracadabra!"

"Say, that's not bad. Where'd you hide it? In the pocket of your khaki pants?"

"And now the great Eisengrim will make it reappear ..."

"Eisengrim? Where you'd get a name like that?"

"And are you supposed to squirm so much?"

"Uh, wait a moment. The great Eisengrim is experiencing technical problems and must briefly vacate the stage ..."

"Hah! He broke the egg!"

"O wise and mighty Eisengrim, if you're so anxious to have your eggs scrambled, why not use a skillet instead of the inside of your trousers?"

Little did his brothers know. Despite these early failures in magic, in his adulthood Davies would become a master magician of a different sort.

2

Youth

If a boy can't have a good teacher, give him a psychological cripple or an exotic cripple to cope with; don't just give him a bad, dull teacher.
(*Fifth Business*)

There are no great performances without great audiences.... Great theatre, great music-drama, is created again and again on both sides of the footlights.
(*The Lyre of Orpheus*)

"You sowed the seeds of Robertson's interest in books and theatre," Zadkiel spoke. "But did you have to make him miserable, in school and with his mother?"

Fred, Florence, Arthur, Robertson, and Rupert Davies. Kingston, 1926.

"A man won't get far if he doesn't take a few knocks. I would have thought you knew that about humans," Maimas said, snuffling slightly.

"But good relations with one's mother are crucial, Maimas. When this bond turns sour ..."

"You're quite right, Zadkiel. Davies will suffer because of his mother, but this suffering will inspire him. An artist is like an omelette, old boy. You have to crack his eggs if he's going to assume the right consistency."

"But surely you didn't keep him in that hovel Renfrew for long?"

"It wasn't such a bad place. Still, it had served its purpose and I shoved Robertson on, as you'll see for yourself."

A lways on the lookout for new business opportunities, Rupert decided to purchase the *Daily British Whig* in 1925. This meant moving the family to Kingston, Ontario, which was a more attractive place of residence than Thamesville or Renfrew. As Upper Canada's chief administrative and business centre in the mid-nineteenth century, Kingston was home to Queen's University and the prestigious Royal Military College. It was also nicknamed the Limestone City because of the limestone architectural gems it contained. All in all it was a sophisticated town, by Canadian standards, and would introduce Davies to rich offerings of theatre, music, and art. Down the road, too, it would serve as the setting for Davies's Salterton Trilogy.

When Rupert decided within a year of his arrival to purchase the city's second paper, the *Kingston Daily Standard*, and amalgamate it with the *Daily British Whig* to produce the *Kingston Whig-Standard*, the prosperous Robertson household became an even wealthier one. Rupert moved his family into Calderwood, a large villa-like house that was equipped with all the modern amenities and surrounded by an immense, well-tended garden (the latter would figure prominently in Davies's first novel, *Tempest-Tost*). The property was even haunted: the ghost of Dr. Betts, a former owner who allegedly drowned his daughter in a bathtub, paraded itself before a group of guests. And the witch from his childhood continued to dog him.

"You're here!" he muttered in fury one night as the witch's malevolent form assumed a position near his bed. "I thought I left you behind in Renfrew, you bitch!"

Davies attended early high school at the Kingston Collegiate Institute. As would be his practice in later years, he startled his peers with his unusual mode of dress: outlandish ties, an old-fashioned jacket, and a purple handkerchief. He also entered his school's numerous writing contests for poetry, fiction, and historical essays, and frequently walked away with first prize. And then there were the school's theatrical productions, which Davies now could not get his fill of — plays such as *The Merchant of Venice* and R.B. Sheridan's *The School for Scandal* — and in which he worked exceedingly hard to get his "technique" perfect. Theatre had become his greatest passion since he had travelled to Toronto and seen the famous D'Oyly Carte Opera Company's production of Gilbert and Sullivan's *Mikado*. For the first time in his life he grasped how brilliant staging, inventive set design, and magnificent costumes could transport an audience.

"What part did you like best?" Rupert asked as he and his son left the Royal Alexandra Theatre. Oblivious to the chill winter air, Davies was humming the song "Three Little Maids."

"I liked all of it. One day I want to live in a world like that."

"In Titipu, Japan? I'm afraid that's quite impossible ..."

"I meant in the theatre. There can't be anything finer than to be an actor."

"Let's not get carried away. I like theatre too, Bobbie, but there's the real world to consider and a living to be made."

"But the theatre *is* real. It's what the world is like when adults stop pretending and show their true behaviour. In fact, the stage is more real than the real world itself."

"I see. And what about your future salary?"

"You saw the crowds lined up at the doors. You also said how beastly hard it was to buy tickets for the show. Some actors must be making an excellent living!"

Now that Davies was fifteen, Rupert wished to set him on the path to success and pressed him to write the entrance exam for Upper Canada College in Toronto. Founded in 1829, UCC was modelled on English residential schools like Eton and Harrow and was itself Canada's foremost private school. Its mandate was to provide its students with a rigorous mental and physical education (and has produced a long roster of distinguished Canadians, including Ted Rogers, Galen Weston, Michael Ignatieff, Conrad Black, and, of course, Robertson Davies himself). Not only did Davies easily pass the exam, but he qualified for a handsome entrance scholarship; the headmaster, W.L. "Choppy" Grant, however, decided to give the award to a less fortunate student, much to Davies's distress and indignation.

The school posed certain challenges. First, there was the chronic lack of privacy: bathing took place in a common space, the toilets sat in booths with no doors on them, and it was strictly forbidden to spend time on one's own. The discipline, too, was tough and confronted students with innumerable rules which they, as future gentlemen, were obligated to observe: standing when a master entered the room, raising one's hat when passing a master, observing the dress code, avoiding slang in one's speech, and other limits on "vulgar" practices. Finally, in contrast to Davies's detestation of physical exercise, the school took great pride in its athletics program.

On the other hand, the faculty consisted of well-educated and experienced gentlemen and scholars, many of whom had peculiar quirks. Mr. Darnill always kept a boxing glove handy, which was filled with a heavy substance. If a student acted up, he would toss this glove at the culprit, deliver him a thorough bruising, then draw the glove back by a string on its end. Commander de Marbois, the geography teacher, had sailed around the world and was rumoured to have practised cannibalism with the natives of Tierra del Fuego (he would figure later in Davies's novel *The Cunning Man* as the philosophizing Jock Daubigny). Mr. Parlee and Mr. Potter had both served with distinction in the Great War and been gravely wounded — occasionally Mr. Potter would climb the pipes in his classroom. Students knew far better than to laugh.

The school would later figure in Davies's novels as the ubiquitous Colborne College, of which Davies would write the following in his last novel, *The Cunning Man*, through his character Jonathan Hullah:

> I am sick to death of writers who whine about their school-days. Let's get it over with: the food was dreadful and the living accommodation was primitive, but we knew we weren't there to enjoy life, but to be prepared for its rigours, and on the whole I think it was a good program.... A boy who can go through a first-rate boarding-school and emerge in one piece is ready for most of what the world is likely to bring him.

Certainly Davies found his niche in this environment. Repeating his flamboyancy from his days at Kingston Collegiate Institute, Davies stunned his peers by dressing up in jackets and collars that deviated from the norm. He even took to wearing a cape and monocle, and studied recordings of a distinguished English actor to shape his Canadian accent into a mid-Atlantic one — he would speak with this same accent for the remainder of his life. With training, too, his manner of speech grew polished, as if each utterance had been rehearsed many hours in advance. Normally he would have been mocked for these eccentricities, and his utter disregard for anything athletic, had he not been a formidable student, a keen speaker, and a more than able participant in the school's drama society. Obsessed with the world of theatre still, he won leading roles in a series of UCC Gilbert and Sullivan productions.

"How are you enjoying our version of *Iolanthe*?" Headmaster Grant asked Edward Wodson, drama critic for the *Toronto Evening Telegram*.

"I have to be truthful, Choppy," Wodson replied. "I loathe high school theatrical productions and consented to attend tonight only because you twisted my arm. But ..."

"Yes?"

"Well, I can't take my eyes off that student who's playing Major-General Stanley."

"His name is William Robertson Davies. He's quite good, isn't he?"

"Remarkable, I would say. His diction is faultless and his timing is superb. He will earn his bread and butter in the liberal arts, if he is so minded."

Davies *was* gifted in the humanities. He was much more widely read than the typical UCC student, and every day only furthered the gap. Besides his fascination with Dickens, whom he read and reread, he was powerfully attracted to the novelist Aldous Huxley (best known for his dystopian work *Brave New World*) and the British playwright George Bernard Shaw. Within the English and History classroom, at least, he was regularly given assignments that far surpassed normal curriculum requirements. Understanding that his words would not be wasted on young Davies, Headmaster Grant took him on a private walk one day and recounted to him the ins and outs of the late-nineteenth-century Oscar Wilde scandal. And of course, Davies contributed regularly to the school paper, the *College Times*. Here is an example of his writing — a poem that was written at the age of seventeen:

> For school masters, in fairness it be told
> Must pander to young fools instead of old,
> Yet old fools too, they must perforce assuage
> For parents plague the poor, distracted sage;
> "Is Willy well?" "How long is Nolly's bed?"
> "Is Dick a favourite?" "When is Percy fed?"
> While boys, like hogs, spurn each scholastic pearl
> Which in their path the febrile ushers hurl.
> O Masters, men born free, but self-enslaved
> Upon your mossy tombs this verse be graved;
> "Restrain thy tears, whoe'er shall tread this sod
> Here lives a man who tried to be a god;
> God-like, but human he employed his years
> Trying to make silk bags from porcine ears."

His efforts, so precocious and outstanding for their literary sparkle, attracted the notice of B.K. Sandwell, a UCC graduate and editor of *Saturday Night*, Canada's foremost weekly paper about public affairs and the arts; down the road he would hire Davies to work for his publication.

Despite his talents and success in literature, however, Davies still proved hopelessly inept in mathematics, much to his frustration. His weakness in this area was only compounded by the impatience of his teacher, Mr. McKenzie.

"All right. Who can provide us with the slope for the line described in the linear equation, y= -3x + 16? Davies, we haven't heard from you in a while."

"I have no idea, sir."

"No idea? The answer's staring you in the face, man, and you have no idea?"

"It's all a great big muddle, sir."

"I sometimes think you're hiding your ability, Davies. Because if you aren't, you're the most blundering student I've ever encountered. Your average in this course can best be expressed by a negative number."

"No doubt, sir."

"Very well. I'll ask someone else. But be warned, Davies. Without your math matriculation, you cannot attend university."

"I'm aware of that, sir."

"That means you're doomed to navigate the ignorant masses, Davies."

"I'll do my best to prove you wrong, sir."

But Mr. McKenzie was partially right. When Davies graduated from UCC in 1932, he did not have sufficient high school credits to be accepted into a university program, and all because he had failed mathematics. To distract him from this educational impasse, and always happy to have his youngest son around him, his father brought him on a trip to Europe that summer. Unlike many businessmen whose investments had faltered in the wake of the stock market crash in 1929, Rupert had been able to preserve his wealth through the course of the Depression. In fact, his principal reason for travelling abroad was to procure himself an estate in Wales, which he was now rich enough to visit on an annual basis. With Davies's approval, he wound up purchasing Fronfraith Hall, a sizeable estate some ten miles distant from his place of birth, Welshpool. In England, Davies had other concerns.

He gorged himself on theatre. Every night he attended plays at Stratford and Malvern, maximizing his enjoyment by reading the script in advance. He also attended lectures on the theatre and began collecting Victorian plays and books on theatrical production — over his lifetime he would amass a library on this subject of over four thousand volumes. By the time he returned to Canada, his appetite for the dramatic arts, far from being satisfied, was near insatiable.

There still remained the problem of acceptance into university. Convinced his son belonged in a university setting, Rupert made full use of his many connections and finally met with success. Davies was admitted into Queen's University for a three-year course of study as a special student, with the proviso that he would not receive a degree on graduation.

"So, I won't be navigating the ignorant masses after all," he whispered to himself on receiving the news.

Despite his "inferior" ranking, Davies created an impression on campus. Articulate, immensely well-read, with his crisp, British intonation and unusual mode of dress — expensive tweed jackets with leather patches on the elbows, purple ties, and a lavish cape — he was often taken by students to be a faculty member. His course of study was obvious. He continued with his

English studies, read a lot of history, and immersed himself in German and Russian literature. At the suggestion of a psychology professor, George Humphrey, he also familiarized himself with Havelock Ellis's monumental *Studies in the Psychology of Sex.*

"What's that book I see you toting everywhere?" his mother asked when he came home late one evening. His brother Fred was sitting with her.

"It's part of a series that was written by a psychologist and medical doctor, Havelock Ellis."

"I've heard of him," Fred broke in. "He writes a lot of smut."

"I believe a more accurate description is that Dr. Ellis has written compendiously on the diversity of sexual relations among humans."

"He writes about queers," Fred jeered. "He thinks such horrible relations are normal. It's a good thing Dad never paid to have me schooled like you, not if it means I have to admire freaks like Havelock Ellis."

"Fred has a point, Bobbie. Why are you wasting your time reading such filth? I'm surprised the university would allow its students to handle such material."

"I'm a student of the human condition. If I want to understand my fellow citizen, then I have to observe him in all his manifestations. And far from being censured, Dr. Ellis should be commended for his honesty and scholarship."

"Now I know why Queen's won't grant you a degree when you leave," his brother said with a spiteful laugh. "Even if you speak like an English ponce."

While Davies contributed sporadically to the Queen's University journal, *The Bookshelf*, he was (as always) active on the theatrical front. Whether it was as producer, director, set designer, or actor (or a combination of all four) he involved himself in productions of *Alice in Wonderland, The Importance of Being Earnest, A Midsummer Night's Dream,* and *Oedipus, King of Thebes.* In the case of Sophocles' tragedy, which was not known to general audiences at the time, Davies decided on a lavishly visual spectacle.

"The thing about Greek tragedy, Bob, is that it is always muted and never shocks the audience," Wilhelmina Gordon, a professor of English, advised him. "All violence is suggested and remains offstage."

"That might have worked in ancient Greece, but I have different ideas."

"I hesitate to ask. Like what?"

"In the last episode, when Oedipus appears before the citizens of Thebes, he's blinded himself."

"That's right."

"Well, I want him to be dripping with blood. And I want the women on stage...."

"The ones you've dressed up in those scanty costumes?"

"Yes. I want some of them to scream as soon as he walks on. That should get a rise from people."

"That's not true to the spirit of Greek drama."

"My purpose is to dazzle, and you can never go wrong with sex and violence."

It was through his theatrical pursuits, *Alice in Wonderland* in particular, that Davies got his first taste of the Sweezey family in late 1933. Mrs. Harriet Sweezey, the daughter of a Queen's philosophy professor, was in a rocky marriage with Robert Sweezey, a brilliant survey engineer. Impressed with Davies's production of *Alice,* she invited him to Pine Ledge, the family's lavish country house, for a week-long New Year's party to produce *The Importance of Being Earnest.* On meeting her youngest daughter, eighteen-year-old Eleanor, Davies was bowled over.

"I'd be careful around Eleanor, if I were you," Mrs. Sweezey advised him.

"Why's that?"

"She's capable of cruelty. If she senses she has you wrapped around her finger, she won't treat you well."

"She seems very decent to me."

"Don't say I didn't warn you."

If anything, Mrs. Sweezey's words spurred Davies on. Through the course of the spring of 1934, he and Eleanor spent lots of time together. Davies was a regular guest at Pine Ledge, and the pair often went on drives, attended plays and concerts, or sat in on Sunday evening services — not to listen to the sermon, but to enjoy each other's company. Over the next year both participated in Queen's productions of the fifteenth-century morality play *Everyman* and Shakespeare's *A Midsummer Night's Dream* (staged on Rupert's magnificent lawns). When Davies joined his father in Wales that summer, he wrote regularly (and affectionately) to Eleanor back home.

She was not the first of Davies's girlfriends. Not long before his introduction to Eleanor, Davies had been infatuated with Elizabeth Stewart, whom he had practically overwhelmed with his conversation and interests — only to lose her to a Royal Military College cadet. Because he had grown up in a household without women (besides his mother) and had spent a large part of his adolescence in an all-boys school, Davies was possibly a bit "pushy" with the women who attracted him. Despite their glorious times together — Davies was always amusing and full of boundless energy — Eleanor was impatient with Davies's endless attentions and would occasionally keep him waiting or fail to show up for a date.

"I don't mean to say I told you so," Harriet Sweezey observed one night when Davies appeared to take Eleanor to a dance, only to discover she had gone with someone else, "but I told you so. Eleanor can be cruel."

"She'll come around eventually."

"I wouldn't be so sure of that."

In the spring of 1935, Davies's tenure at Queen's University reached an end. Despite the courses he had taken and his formal attainment of a B.A., he could not receive a degree because of his special-student status. Just as he was trying to puzzle out his next career step, he received heartening news. Some months earlier, at the suggestion of one of his professors, he had sent in an application to Balliol College in Oxford, England. Because he had not received any response, he assumed Oxford had rejected him. In the late summer, however, his father cabled him from England to announce that he had in fact been admitted into the B.A. program. Davies started packing for this adventure overseas, but first he was determined to seal his relationship with Eleanor.

"I'll be gone two years. But when I return with a degree in hand, I'll be able to work as a drama professor."

"That's so exciting, Bob. Congratulations."

"The thing is, I don't want to lose you in the shuffle. That's why, after intense deliberation, I ... well ... that is ... Look — will you marry me when I get back?"

"Oh Bob. I don't know. I'm not so sure that's a good idea."

"Why not? You know me well by now ..."

"To begin with, there's madness in my family. Look at my uncle — do you remember how he attacked you once? And there are certain other relatives as well."

"Don't be ridiculous. Every family has its genetic quirks. My side suffers from asthma, frazzled nerves, and Welsh garrulity ..."

"And I don't love you."

"Oh. That's more serious. But ... is there someone else you love?"

"No, not at present."

"Well, why don't we leave matters as follows: I'll go abroad, I'll write regularly, I'll visit in the summers and ... maybe you can wait for me."

"Yes, that sounds like a workable arrangement."

"Good. And take my word for it: everything will work out well."

But even as he kissed his "sweetheart" goodbye and prepared for his long, transatlantic journey, Davies experienced a pang of doubt.

Davies, at the age of twenty-two, acting as stage manager of a production of Richard III. *Oxford, February, 1936.*

3

Merry Old England

Education in England spoils so many Canadians
— except Rhodes scholars, who come back and
get Government jobs right away.
(*Tempest-Tost*)

The characteristic of the artist is discontent.
Universities may produce fine critics, but not
artists. We are wonderful people, we university
people, but we are apt to forget the limitations
of learning, which cannot create or beget.
(*The Rebel Angels*)

Wars are national and international disasters,
but everyone in a warring nation fights a war

of his own and sometimes it cannot be decided
whether he has won or lost.
(*What's Bred in the Bone*)

"I didn't know you were so capricious, Maimas. Robertson's first two
decades contain so many fits and false starts that the poor creature
doesn't have a clue who he is. He dresses like someone from a
bygone age, he corrupts his native speech with a British inflection,
and he seems most at peace with himself when he's acting out some
role on stage."

"You're sharp as ever, my dear fellow. At this point Robertson is a
shaky construction — he's like a house that's been jumbled together
with such an ungainly mix of materials that one good blast and he'll be
smashed to pieces."

"So that's why you introduced him to that woman Eleanor?"

"Top of the class, Zadkiel. She's the blast of wind that will raze
his foundations. But understand that without these upsets Robertson
might have ended up rich, insufferable, and small-town ordinary. Instead he'll be given a very sound knocking and from the wreckage,
soon enough, a magician of words will emerge."

"You seem to relish these acts of vandalism, Maimas."

"I do indeed, Zadkiel, because in my own way I too am a consummate artist."

After a smooth crossing of the Atlantic on the *Empress of
Britain*, Davies landed in England and took up residence
in Oxford. Much to his satisfaction, Balliol was "authentic."
Founded in 1263 as an act of penance on the part of the noble-
man John de Balliol (who had assaulted a bishop), Balliol was
one of Oxford's oldest colleges, with roots that extended into

medieval times. At every turn it was impossible to avoid the institution's age and venerability. The central quad and old library dated back to the early fifteenth century; the traditional annual dinner for Balliol senior students had been started in 1550; and the Snell annual dinner had been established in the late seventeenth century. Distinguished for its high academic standards, Balliol had hosted a long line of eminent thinkers: the economist Adam Smith, two-time Nobel Prize winner Linus Pauling, the Victorian cultural critic Matthew Arnold, folklorist Andrew Lang, three prime ministers (Macmillan, Asquith, and, later, Edward Heath), Canada's governor general Vincent Massey, the historian Arnold Toynbee, the writers Aldous Huxley and Graham Greene, and dozens of other movers and shakers. And what was true of Balliol was true of Oxford as a whole. Davies was at the epicentre of Western culture.

As interesting as his location was, the times were even more earth-shattering. Two years prior to Davies's arrival in England, Adolf Hitler had been elected Reich Chancellor of Germany and was intent on reversing the humiliation of the Versailles Treaty (which had ended the First World War on disadvantageous terms for the defeated Germans) and restoring Germany to its former military prowess. In the spring of 1935, Hitler had re-introduced conscription, in defiance of the strictures of Versailles. And even as Davies was settling down in Oxford, the Führer was inaugurating the Nuremberg Laws, which would strip German Jews of their basic rights and liberties. Davies had a front-row seat to the greatest drama of the twentieth century.

Not that he paid much attention to this storm front. His new setting and course of study left him little time to worry about events to the east. To complete his B.A. he would have to write examinations in Anglo-Saxon, Latin, ancient drama, and

English drama. While strong in these last two subjects, he was weak in the first two and would have to push very hard if he wished to succeed. Certainly his instructors set an impressively high standard. His tutor, Roy Ridley, who served his students cocktails through the course of his tutorials, was the editor of a new series of Shakespeare's plays; J.R.R. Tolkien, who would win fame in the 1950s for his *Lord of the Rings*, lectured Davies on Anglo-Saxon history and literature; and the future author of *The Chronicles of Narnia*, C.S. Lewis, also lectured to Davies on several occasions.

In addition to his studies, Davies involved himself in Oxford's busy social life. As had been his custom previously, he raised eyebrows with his elaborate manner of dress (wide-brimmed hats, an ostentatious ring, a monocle, and a walking stick). His big personality and natural charisma attracted an array of students to his lodgings, among them Lionel Massey, whose father Vincent had attended Balliol and would play an important role in Davies's future. And then there were the various societies he joined — ones dedicated to arts, history, and literature — where Davies presented talks and essays on a wide spectrum of topics.

His biggest love was the theatre, of course, and much to his satisfaction he was accepted as a member of the Oxford University Dramatic Society (OUDS). This society staged two productions a year, which, in addition to attracting students and faculty members, involved top-ranked theatre people as well. The OUDS version of Shakespeare's *Richard II*, for example, starred Vivien Leigh (who would later play Scarlett O'Hara in *Gone with the Wind*) and was directed by the world-renowned John Gielgud.

Unfortunately, Davies's first year was not a rousing success. His tutor Ridley had assigned him the wrong Latin texts to master, and Davies had never been a fan of Anglo-Saxon literature. Much to his horror and shame — he dreaded disappointing his father, who had gone to great lengths to procure his acceptance into Oxford — he failed both examinations in the spring of 1936. To compound his sense of failure, his relationship with Eleanor took a drastic turn for the worse.

Since his departure from Canada, Davies had written to Eleanor on a daily basis. Whereas he was unambiguous about his feelings for her, she was still reluctant to commit herself to him. A trip home at Christmas had not brought him any closer to his goal of marriage, and when Eleanor spurned his suggestion that she join him in Wales for the summer of 1936, he vented his frustration in a string of letters. She responded accordingly.

> Dear Bob,
> You have expressed impatience with my deci-
> sion not to accompany you to Wales and clearly
> feel I'm trying to avoid you. While this isn't
> quite true — I always look forward to the time
> we spend together — I must confess that I often
> question our long term compatibility with one
> another.
>
> Consider our very different passions. I adore
> mathematics — it happens to be my major here
> at Queen's — while you have no interest in the
> subject whatsoever. I'm not terribly musical,
> while you love attending concerts and singing
> old consort songs. I dance, and you don't. And
> then there's the theatre which you're crazy
> about, while I admit it leaves me cold. Love isn't
> enough to sustain a couple over a lifetime; man

and wife must have common interests as well. If not, they will eventually tire of each other, and estrangement will inevitably settle in.

There is also your personality to consider. I know you don't intend anything by it, but at times you are so cynical that your remarks and conversation leave me feeling confused. I don't understand your need to show off, to dress flamboyantly and dominate the conversation. I'm sure these characteristics are mainly due to your family's influence — if I had been raised around your parents' dinner table, my humour would be as biting as yours — but life with you would test my patience and, over time, my affections would fail.

For these reasons, and after long and hard reflection on the matter, I must conclude that we are not suitable as husband and wife. Furthermore, I have reached the decision that we can no longer see each other and ask you not to correspond with me in future.

I'm very sorry to disappoint you so, but down the road you will understand it's all for the best. Please take care of yourself and enjoy what remains of your stay at Oxford.

Sincerely,
Eleanor

Eleanor's rejection of him, together with his disastrous academic performance, pushed Davies into a tailspin. He was greatly distressed and developed a severe, persistent cough. On the advice of a doctor (Raymond Greene, brother of the novelist Graham Greene) he travelled to his father's estate in Wales for a period of convalescence. There, he was visited by his former Queen's psychology professor, Dr. George Humphrey, who advised him to see one of England's top psychiatrists in London, Dr. Robert Gillespie. Not knowing how else to treat his misery, Davies agreed.

"Listen," Gillespie told him, after several lengthy consultations. "Last session we agreed that life with Eleanor would have been a disaster and she was wise to reject you."

"Yes. Although it pains me to admit as much."

"But why did you pursue her with such pathological intent? I say 'pathological' because your desire for this woman has undermined your health."

"I'm not sure."

"Maybe the answer lies in your family history; in particular, your relationship with your parents. You've told me that you are the youngest child by ten years."

"That's correct."

"Well, is it any wonder that they raised you so disastrously? You were born when both of them were past their childrearing years. You disrupted their routines and they resented the intrusion, hence the many occasions when they forced you to bow down to your mother. Your parents' frustration, moreover, explains their cynicism on the one hand and compensating overprotectiveness on the other."

"And Eleanor ...?"

"That episode can be boiled down to a typical anima projection. Instead of absorbing the anima or universal feminine traits into your ego, you projected these onto Eleanor and therefore found her irresistible."

"I see."

"No, you don't. But you will if you start reading Sigmund Freud."

"Freud?"

"Yes, start with his *Interpretation of Dreams*. I strongly suspect it's just your cup of tea."

Slowly but surely, Davies returned to normal, and digested Eleanor's rejection of him. Indeed, he quickly reached a humane and mature assessment of his former sweetheart, as he explained years later in his novel *The Cunning Man*. Here is Jonathan Hullah commenting on the affair between Julia (a stand-in for Eleanor) and Brocky Gilmartin (a stand-in for himself):

> Looking back, I see how callowly I judged the affair. Julia was not a heartless flirt, as I supposed; she was just a girl testing her powers, which were not inconsiderable, and she was not burdened with any unusual understanding of other people's feelings. As for Brocky, he had perhaps read too much, drunk too much poetry, and was unable to bring his protective cynicism, which served him so well in other matters, to bear on his obsession with Julia. Fortune, who dearly loves such tricks, was having a little sport with them both, and Fortune may show a Chaucerian roughness when she cracks jokes.

On his return to Oxford the following term, Davies was practically restored to normal. Tutor Ron Ridley adjusted his program so that he would pursue a B.Litt. — a research degree — rather than the more difficult B.A. This meant there would be no more Latin or Anglo-Saxon. Ridley even proposed a thesis topic: "Were the female roles in Shakespeare's dramas influenced by the convention that boys had to play them?"

Taking Gillespie up on his suggestion, Davies studied Freud's theory of psychoanalysis. His contention that the mind's unconscious aspect served as a repository of instinctual needs and desires appealed greatly to Davies's imagination. The idea, too, that there was a hidden facet to humans that influenced their actions and revealed their fundamental traits fit in neatly with Davies's assumption that there was a reality deeper than the one that greeted the eye, a wealth of experience that good theatre, for all its artificiality, could elucidate for the right kind of audience. And having always enjoyed a rich and vivid dream life, Davies admired Freud's suggestion that dreams are a key to understanding aspects of one's conscious life — ones that prove so destabilizing or threatening that they are buried deep below one's personality. His reading of Freud, and his assimilation of Freud's theories, would continue for many years.

Naturally, Davies re-enlisted with the OUDS. Graduating from stage manager to treasurer to actor, he honed his understanding of all aspects of the theatre, even as he involved himself in first-rate productions of *Macbeth*, *Twelfth Night*, *The Taming of the Shrew*, and *As You Like It*. In the course of working on the latter, Davies was introduced to Brenda Newbold, an Australian who was studying drama at the Old Vic Theatre. At one point in their first conversation, he offered her his plate of bacon and eggs. She declined, not knowing what his intentions were. Neither thought much of this initial meeting and would have been shocked to discover that they would be spending most of their lives together.

In the late spring of 1938, Davies finally completed his thesis, "Shakespeare's Boy Actors," and submitted it to a panel of examiners. He was worried that his efforts would be rejected — he vomited twice before his examination — but he should have known better. He had been reading Shakespeare and thinking about the staging of his plays since his early adolescence. He had also acted in numerous Shakespeare dramas and, through his experience at Upper Canada College, where Shakespeare's plays had been populated exclusively by schoolboy actors, had witnessed for himself how boys assumed the roles of female characters. His examiners recognized the high quality of his work and not only granted him a pass, but recommended that his thesis be published. Two weeks later he graduated from Oxford with the promised B.Litt.

"How's that for someone who was doomed to navigate the ignorant masses?" he crowed to the imaginary spectre of Mr. McKenzie.

Now that his university days were over, he had to find himself employment. It had taken him three years to clinch a two-year degree, and his personal expenses were mounting. Besides the cost of living at Oxford, Davies had been busy collecting books and old theatre scripts. These activities had cost a fair amount of money, which his father had provided, but not without some hemming and hawing.

Davies also wondered whether he should remain in England. Despite his lack of interest in politics, it was impossible to ignore the developments on the continent. Two years earlier, in 1936, Adolf Hitler had remilitarized the Rhineland — this was German territory that bordered on France and, in the wake of the First World War, had been cleared of a German military presence to facilitate the enforcement of the Versailles Treaty's terms. In this same year, Hitler had involved German troops in the Spanish Civil War — a showdown between Republican Spaniards (supported by socialist and communist volunteers from an array of nations) and fascist forces under General Franco (aided by Germany and Benito Mussolini's Italy). In March of 1938, moreover, while Davies had been agonizing over his thesis, the *Anschluss* (or annexation) of Austria by Germany had occurred, significantly increasing the amount of territory Adolf Hitler commanded. Further German expansion was expected.

Notwithstanding these political eruptions, Davies felt optimistic about his personal future. His thesis was published by J.M. Dent and Sons of London and, while hardly a bestseller, it did receive some positive reviews. With these in hand, Davies set about looking for work as an actor, confident his new book would create a reputation for him in the theatre world.

The world scene only worsened, however, with the outbreak of the Sudetenland Crisis. In the late summer of 1938, Hitler insisted that the Sudetenland — the western district of Czechoslovakia — belonged to Germany and should be annexed. His claims led to the Munich Conference at which Germany, France, and England forced Czechoslovakia to consent to the secession of the Sudetenland and its immediate occupation by German forces. The Munich Accord further stipulated that the Sudetenland marked the end of Hitler's foreign acquisitions. Indeed, on his return to England in early October 1938, British prime minister Neville Chamberlain displayed a copy of the Munich Accord to a crowd before 10 Downing Street and declared it was "peace for our time." He would regret these words a mere six months later.

In contrast to the international scene, Davies's luck was on the rise. In the aftermath of the Sudetenland Crisis, an offer fell his way from out of the blue. Tyrone Guthrie, director of the Old Vic Theatre, had seen Davies perform in the OUDS production of *Twelfth Night* the year before and, impressed with his abilities together with his recent book, invited him to join his theatre company.

"You'd be a jack-of-all-trades, so to speak," Guthrie said as they discussed the offer over pints of beer. "You'll do some acting — the smaller roles for now — and will serve as the company's dramaturge."

"So, you'll want me to arrange the company's program and smooth over the rough passages in the plays we perform?"

"That's about it. And you'll lecture the staff on the history of theatre, production, staging, that sort of thing."

"That sounds wonderful. But why me?"

"There's that book of yours, on boy actors in Shakespeare — very useful stuff in there. At the same time, you're an interesting mix. I like the way you speak, your choice of words, and your oversized perspective. You're possibly that rarest of creatures: an original thinker. Your personality's rough, but I can live with that. So, do we have a deal?"

"We had a deal the moment you phoned."

His job with the Old Vic brought him in contact again with Brenda Newbold. Affected with the same theatre "bug" as Davies, she had been with the company for over two years and had worked her way from assistant stage manager to full stage manager — an unusual feat for a woman at that time. Like Davies, she came from a distant part of the Commonwealth, had grown up in a wealthy household, and, although bright, had not flowered academically because she had suffered all her days from dyslexia. Their similarities led them to become fast friends. And because Brenda was living in London with her divorced mother and sister, Davies was soon a regular member of the Newbold household.

"Your mother's divorced?" Davies asked as he and Brenda dined in a Chinese restaurant while discussing a play they had just taken in.

"Twice divorced, as a matter of fact. My father was an idealist — his name is Paul Mathews. My mother met him at Cambridge, from which he graduated with a degree in mathematics. When the Great War broke out, my father decided he was a conscientious objector and moved my mother to Tasmania — that's Australia's southernmost state — where he was determined to become an apple farmer."

"That sounds romantic."

"And very unrealistic. My mother was used to comfort. She couldn't take the isolation or the hardship of a farming life. When I was two and my sister Maisie was four, she left my father. She remarried after that, and divorced her second husband as well."

"That's rough. How did you become so interested in theatre?"

"I was at my boarding school and was feeling terribly homesick when I was taken to some theatrical production. The sets and costumes were so beautiful that I thought the events on stage were how the world was meant to be."

"That's very odd. For years I've believed the very same thing."

"Do you believe in ghosts?"

"How can't I believe in ghosts?" he answered with a grimace, thinking of the witch who had plagued him for so long, even at Oxford on the odd occasion. "I've witnessed them myself."

"Oh. Well. It's getting late. Let's call for the bill."

"Don't worry. I'll look after it."

"That's ridiculous. I'm paying for myself. I work in the same place as you and know exactly what your salary is. It isn't enough for you to foot both bills on your own."

Davies was transported. He was appreciated by the company's younger members for his extensive knowledge of the history of theatre. He was surrounded by a crowd of old actors whose recollections of players from a bygone age entertained him endlessly and filled in the cracks in his knowledge of Victorian actors and stage techniques. He found Tyrone Guthrie's expertise and creativity a bottomless source of inspiration. And he was delighted with the occasional acting job that came his way in plays by Shakespeare, Shaw, and Oliver Goldsmith.

Most important, his friendship with Brenda deepened. When finished at the theatre, the pair would often attend another company's production, then sit together afterwards to analyze the play's weaknesses and strengths. Davies often walked Brenda home, where their conversation and antics would continue in her family's sitting room.

Unfortunately, there were dark spots.

"You're Robertson Davies, aren't you?" someone asked at a party.

"Yes, and you are ...?"

"Lionel Hale, theatre critic for the *Daily Mail*."

"I read your column regularly."

"I'm delighted to hear it. And I have been watching you closely since you started working for Tyrone. In fact ..."

"Yes?"

"Well, you're a competent actor, but nothing brilliant. On the other hand you have a vast knowledge of theatre and a facility with words. Have you ever considered writing plays rather than acting in them?"

"Well, I've dabbled at the writing aspect ..."

"I'm glad to hear it. Because if you leave the stage of your own free will you'll save me the chore of having to savage you in public. Just so you know."

Much more ominously, Adolf Hitler finally pushed the Western alliance too far. In the spring of 1939, he directed his troops to conquer the rest of Czechoslovakia, in complete violation of the Munich Accord. The leaders of France and England delivered Hitler an ultimatum: if he attacked Poland (his next obvious target) he would precipitate a war. Neville Chamberlain and Édouard Daladier assumed that Hitler would avoid invading Poland because such aggression would provoke a counterattack from Russia. Much to their shock, however, Joseph Stalin (the Russian leader) and Hitler signed a non-aggression treaty, the Molotov-Ribbentrop Pact, on August 24, 1939. A week later, on September 1, German troops poured over the western Polish border. On September 3, Chamberlain's government declared war on Germany. Conservative MP Winston Churchill, who was destined to become prime minister eight months later, delivered the following remarks that day to the House of Commons:

> This is not a question of fighting for Danzig or fighting for Poland. We are fighting to save the whole world from the pestilence of Nazi tyranny and in defence of all that is most sacred to man. This is no war of domination or imperial aggrandizement or material gain; no war to shut any country out of its sunlight and means of progress. It is a war, viewed in its inherent quality, to establish, on impregnable rocks, the rights of the individual, and it's a war to establish and revive the stature of man.

Because military matters were now a priority, funding to various theatre companies was cut — such funding had never amounted to much to begin with. Davies and Brenda guessed the company would shut down before long and were wondering what their next step should be. They discussed this problem in the town of Buxton (northwest of London) where the company was on tour — London was under a general blackout and Guthrie had decided to move the "operation" out of town.

"We won't get back to normal for a very long time," Brenda sighed as they wandered the town's municipal gardens.

"That means all sorts of actors will be out of work, including yours truly. There's no reason for me to be in England any longer."

"And I'll have to return to Australia, I suppose. I shouldn't be thinking about myself in times like these, but I can't say life in Australia attracts me."

"You do have an alternative, you know. You could come with me to Canada."

"Don't be ridiculous! I have nothing in Canada, no work, no friends, no family ..."

"You would have family. There'd be a husband, and if we were lucky, children down the road — three, I should think. And I wouldn't merely be your husband; I'd be your closest friend. I know it sounds silly, but in my opinion the best of marriages are founded on friendship as much as they're founded on love ..."

"Mr. Robertson Davies! Are you proposing to me?"

"Yes. And you should answer quickly because our next curtain rises in forty minutes."

They continued working with the Old Vic for the next four months until their wedding took place on February 2, 1940. Although no member of Davies's family was present to attend the ceremonies, Rupert sent a reporter and photographer to cover the proceedings. After a month's honeymoon in Wales, the couple eventually travelled to Liverpool where they boarded a ship that would conduct them to Quebec City.

It was a nerve-racking journey. The *sitzkrieg* was still in effect — this was the seven-month period of inactivity on the western front after the initial declaration of war — but allied ships were being hunted by German U-boats in the North Atlantic. The ship sailed with its lights blacked out at night to conceal its presence from German predators on the high seas.

"It's frightening to think they could be cruising beneath us even as we speak."

"It's best not to think of such things."

"They could have us in their sights and their torpedoes at the ready."

"If they hit us, at least we'll die together. Besides ..."

"The sea is cold. I hate the idea of drifting about in ice water."

"In that case, you should take a look over to your right."

"Where ...? Oh my goodness! Are those lights I see?"

"They are. That's your first sight of Canada. Welcome home, my sweet."

Brenda and Robertson after their marriage at the Chelsea Old Church, February 2, 1940.

4

Journalist and Playwright

The marriages that worked best were those in which the unity still permitted of some separateness — not a ranting independence, but a firm possession by both man and woman of their own souls.
(*The Lyre of Orpheus*)

Reading is a form of indulgence, like eating and smoking. Some men smoke heavily and some drink heavily; I read heavily, and sometimes I have the most awful hangovers.
(*One Half of Robertson Davies*)

Marchbanks' Journalistic Training Course was simple: (a) Read all of the Bible, or at

least three-quarters of it, because it is a classical education, a history, and a compen-
dium of ancient wisdom; (b) read the Book
of Common Prayer, as a lesson in style, and
also of good manners toward your superiors
(a grave lack among journalists as a class); (c)
read *The Complete Works of Shakespeare,* for
knowledge of human nature and vocabulary;
(d) read Defoe's *Robinson Crusoe* until you
have mastered his ability to make dubious,
and even imaginary things seem true. Do not
bleat about "the public's right to know" when
you really mean your own right to snoop. But
snoop, all the same, and keep your trap shut
about your sources or they will turn on you
and destroy you.

(*The Table Talk of Samuel Marchbanks*)

"Your methods are peculiar, Maimas. First you disappoint your charge
to the point of madness, then you drop a loving partner in his lap."

"Believe me, Zadkiel, I'm only out for Robertson's best interests.
If I had introduced him to Brenda from the start, he would never have
known the agony of unfulfilled passion, and his later efforts would
have suffered for it."

"And what about his failed theatrical career? I thought you were
going to allow him to take the world by storm?"

"That would have been the easy way out. No, I wanted Robertson
to glimpse the Promised Land but to be immediately denied entrance
to it — again, to spur him on to further efforts. Good actors are
impressive to be sure, but first-rate writers are a scarce commodity.
If he had made his mark with the Old Vic Theatre, he would not have

realized his true potential. But enough talk. Let's start him on his arduous apprenticeship."

"This is just like a movie, old man. A pity we didn't bring any popcorn along."

O n their arrival in Canada, Davies and his wife moved in with his parents in Kingston. They did not have much choice in the matter. They barely had any money between them and did not have good jobs to return to. And within weeks of their arrival Brenda discovered she was pregnant. To complicate matters, life with Davies's parents proved difficult. Always possessive of her youngest son, Florence did not take kindly to his new wife on the scene. And Davies's older brother Fred resented the fact that Brenda liked to borrow Rupert's car — Davies himself had never learned to drive and Brenda was the family chauffeur. It was clear the young couple had to move out on their own, and this meant Davies had to find himself work.

Before he set about seeking employment, there was the matter of military service to look after. In July of the previous year, before war had actually broken out, Davies had written to Vincent Massey, Canada's High Commissioner to London, and offered to serve in some intelligence or propaganda capacity, in the event that bullets started to fly. No one had taken him up on this suggestion. Now that the war was in full swing, Canada was dispatching thousands of men to Britain. While conscription was not yet in effect, the National Resources Mobilization Act required males above the age of eighteen to register for military service, but in Canada alone and not in any foreign setting. In compliance with the law, Davies registered with the authorities but, to his relief and discomfort, was rejected because his eyesight was so terrible. He was free to concentrate on other matters.

When he did seek work, he found it almost effortlessly. Given his formidable writing talents, and Rupert's influence in the newspaper business, it was not long before Davies was writing editorials that appeared in the *Whig-Standard*. The primary purpose of these pieces was to entertain and their subject matter was centred around the arts and literature, as well as any topic that captured Davies's fancy. The general manager of the paper, his brother Arthur, was offended by his lighthearted tone.

"Rob, can I talk to you for a moment about this latest piece of yours, 'Merry-Go-Round'?" his brother asked with a confrontational air.

"It's rather good, isn't it? I think a description of an old-fashioned calliope will bring a smile to our readers' faces."

"Do you have any idea what's happening abroad? Last month at Dunkirk the British army was forced to evacuate France because the German army cut them off. Thirty thousand British troops were killed and another 34,000 were captured. Worse, the Germans now occupy Belgium, Holland, and most of France, in addition to Norway and Denmark. Spain is controlled by the fascist leader Franco, and Switzerland, Sweden, and Ireland are neutral."

"I may not be in the army, but I do read the papers, you know. Incidentally, I thought Churchill's speech in the wake of Dunkirk was masterful. 'We will fight on the beaches, we shall fight on the landing grounds, we shall fight ... um ... in our kitchens and driveways ...'"

"You mean, 'We shall fight in the fields and in the streets, we shall fight in the hills; we shall never surrender!'"

"That's it. For sheer, blood-rousing, gut-stiffening, hard-hammering rhetoric, the Bard himself could do no better."

"But that's my point. The feeling abroad is that England will fall. Even as we speak, the RAF is battling the Luftwaffe to keep the Germans from staging a naval invasion. In other words, this isn't the time for fun and games, but for blood, toil, tears, and sweat, just as Churchill recently proposed. Your story about a merry-go-round is trivial and insulting."

"I couldn't disagree more. People need diversions in troubled times. It's good for their morale. I dare say, Churchill himself would agree."

If Churchill would not have agreed, Rupert certainly did. Indeed, in August 1940, Davies started contributing a regular thrice-weekly column entitled "Cap and Bells" to the *Whig-Standard* and *Peterborough Examiner*, under the name Samuel Marchbanks. This creation of a literary alter ego allowed Davies to express himself more daringly in his writing, with plenty of references to scatology and rude bodily functions, than would have been the case had he been writing in his own name. Like his earlier articles, these Marchbanks pieces discussed theatre, books, and the daily vexations of small-town Ontario life — managing one's furnace, dealing with obstreperous neighbours, tending to one's health and hygiene, or navigating the Canadian weather. Here is Marchbanks, for example, on the proper way of handling a door-to-door salesman:

> As I was slicing some bread this morning there was a ring at my door, and I opened it to find an ugly-faced ruffian with a heavy paunch standing on the mat. "D'yuh own this house or rent it?" he demanded. "Who wants to know?" I asked. "I do," said Pauncho; "this house had oughta be insulated, and if yuh don't own it

there's no good my wastin' time talkin' to yuh." I disembowelled him neatly with the breadknife, and called the Sanitation Department to come and clear away the mess.

And here is Marchbanks again on shaving lotion:

Was talking to a friend of mine, and noticed that he had a strange smell. When I commented on this he blushed becomingly, and said that it was some shaving lotion which he had been given for Christmas. It was manufactured especially for masculine use, and was called (I think he said) "Horse". A number of scents for the male are now on the market and all of them guarantee to make the wearer smell of something wholesome and rugged like heather, or the harness-room in a livery stable. They have short, rugged, masculine names, like "Gym," "Running Shoes," "Barn," "Cheese," "Glue," and the like.

So popular did these columns prove that they were soon the talk of the town in both Kingston and Peterborough. And the longevity of the column was a sign of its success: Davies would continue writing in Marchbanks' voice for a full thirteen years. And with the publication of his column in book form down the road, Samuel Marchbanks would become a household name across Canada.

Despite its warm reception, the Marchbanks column was hardly enough to keep his family going, especially since Davies and Brenda had left the family home in Kingston to set up shop for themselves in Toronto. On the advice of a professor who had helped Davies secure acceptance into Queen's as a special student, Davies paid a visit to the editor of the publishing firm Clarke, Irwin & Company in Toronto. Discovering that he was an expert on the history of theatre, and that he had had his thesis published by a respectable London house, W.H. Clarke asked Davies if he would be willing to write an introductory text to Shakespeare for high school students. Davies readily accepted the offer.

Davies's writing assignments did not stop there. Learning of the death by drowning of the literary editor for *Saturday Night*, Davies applied for the position in October 1940. The editor, B.K. Sandwell, had long ago admired Davies's contributions to the Upper Canada College newsletter, the *College Times*, as well as his *Shakespeare's Boy Actors*, and hired him on the spot. Davies started writing book reviews — a task that required him to read voluminously but, as he would write in a later article, "My great-aunt Isobel Robertson read three books every day for the last twenty-five years of her life, and I am cast in her mould." He also penned monthly theatrical reviews. It was at this time, too, that his daughter Miranda was born — she was named after the character in Shakespeare's *The Tempest* — and Davies was suddenly faced with a novel set of responsibilities. What with his new parental role, his thrice-weekly column for the *Whig-Standard* and *Peterborough Examiner*, and now his review work for *Saturday Night*, Davies was being pulled in all directions. But his journalistic efforts did not stop there.

In December 1941 — two weeks after the Japanese attack on Pearl Harbor — the head editor for the *Peterborough Examiner* died unexpectedly. After careful consideration, Rupert decided that his youngest son should take over this position, not only because he wanted someone whose loyalty he could count on, but because he thought this promotion would benefit his son immensely. At the time, Peterborough was something of a backwater: it had a population of thirty thousand, its citizens were churchgoers and conservative in temperament, and there was little in the way of theatre and culture. Still fresh from his years at Oxford and the Old Vic, Davies was convinced he and Brenda would die for want of oxygen in such a locale.

"There won't be anyone to talk to," he complained to his father at the family Christmas celebration. "These people haven't opened a book in years unless it was to glean some wisdom from the Bible. You're dispatching me to the wilderness, in other words."

"This is a huge promotion, Robbie," Rupert replied, re-filling his snifter with a finger of brandy. "You'll have control of a town paper. You'll supply its news and shape its opinions, although you should temper just how loud you shout in your editorial section."

"And I'll have to quit my post at *Saturday Night.*"

"So? Your salary will be triple what you earn at present. And we'll buy you a house with company funds, which you can rent from us."

"Compared to London, Toronto is enough of a wasteland. But Peterborough ..."

"You went to London and Oxford because of me. It's time to repay me for my investment in you. Don't disappointment me, son."

With little choice in the matter, Davies moved his family to Peterborough in March 1942 — Brenda was now pregnant with their second daughter, Jennifer. As Davies had suspected, their change of locale proved difficult for the first few years.

The local population was not terribly receptive to outsiders (in Davies's eyes at least) and was intimidated by their accents, their cultivation, and their big-city temperament. When the family ate outside on warm summer nights, or Davies strolled about the property in khaki shorts, or espoused his liberal views on a variety of hot-button issues, the townspeople did not know what to think. During a bout of flu that kept him bedridden for three weeks, Davies grew a beard and, admiring the effect, decided to keep it — it became a lifelong badge with him. Together with his elaborate way of dressing, this beard marked him off from the town's clean-shaven males; indeed, people wondered why a strapping man like him was not serving in the army like many of their townsfolk, little realizing his eyesight kept him from such service.

"Hey old man! Didja just come outta the woods or somefin? Ya look like a lumberjack!"

"Naw! That's Rip van Winkle. Hey Rip, mebbe you'll wake up some if we hit ya with some pebbles, eh? Then you can fight the krauts like my old man overseas!"

The sobriety of Peterborough reflected the bleak temper of the outside world. The war was grinding on. By now, the Germans had occupied large parts of Eastern Europe and were wrestling for control of the western half of Russia. With his launch of Operation Barbarossa in 1941, Hitler had enmeshed the German Wehrmacht in a protracted, violent fight to the finish with the Soviet Union's vast Red Army. On the western front, in August 1942, the British authorities had given the green light to the disastrous Operation Jubilee, a mini invasion of Dieppe in northern France that claimed nine hundred Canadian lives and led to the imprisonment of many others. The British were simultaneously fighting hard in Egypt to prevent the Germans from seizing the Suez Canal — final victory in this theatre would only come in 1943 at El Alamein. Nineteen forty-three would also see the start of the brutally fierce Operation Husky — the invasion of Sicily by Canadian, English, and U.S. forces (the latter having joined the war after the Japanese attack on Pearl Harbor). The Canadians alone would suffer some 2,400 casualties in the campaign. Allied forces would gradually gain the upper hand, but the overall carnage was far from over.

If Peterborough did not offer him many social contacts, his routines did keep Davies occupied. In addition to managing various aspects of the paper, he revamped the editorial section and wrote on a wide array of topics: psychology, theatre, literature, education, and religion, in addition to his usual Marchbanks contributions. He sometimes challenged the local authorities when he felt they were failing to uphold their responsibilities. In one editorial, for example, he argued in favour of birth control and antagonized the local Roman Catholic bishop. All this work, which amounted to a full-time job, was only part of his overall journalistic output as he was writing for other publications as well. Indeed, Davies calculated that he was writing twelve thousand words each week at this time.

His workload only continued to grow. Convinced journalism would reduce him to a hack and, no matter how many columns he banged out, would never satisfy his artistic yearnings, Davies composed plays in his spare time — his ultimate ambition being to write for the London stage. His first serious effort, *The King Who Could Not Dream* (1943–44), tells the story of the Anglo-Saxon King Aethelred (968–1016) and the departure of his queen, Emma, on a pilgrimage to Jerusalem. Enslaved by the Caliph Montasir, Emma comes to love her captor because he embodies certain qualities that her own husband — nicknamed

"The Unready" — so conspicuously lacks. Although Davies's old friend and theatre boss Tyrone Guthrie was taken with this strange tale and passed it along to John Gielgud, the script failed to generate any strong enthusiasm and was left to one side.

Undaunted, Davies tried his hand at radio plays. His father owned part of a Toronto radio station and, in 1944, a set of fifteen-minute plays were broadcast, each designed to promote the Victorian Order of Nurses. Some months later Davies wrote another six radio "playlets," whose purpose was to advertise Victory Loan Bonds. The public response was an equal mix of confusion and amusement.

Two serious efforts followed in the spring and summer of 1945: *Hope Deferred* and *A Jig for a Gypsy* (respectively). The former is set in seventeenth-century Quebec and pits two bishops against Frontenac, the governor of Quebec, in a struggle to stage Moliere's play *Tartuffe* (whose central character seems devout but is in truth a scheming hypocrite). *A Jig for a Gypsy* tells the story of a Welsh gypsy who, after revealing the future of a liberal politician, is hounded by a band of conservative rivals, only to be vindicated at play's end. Like *The King Who Could Not Dream*, neither play generated any significant interest.

"Why won't anyone respond to my plays?" Davies complained to Brenda one night. "Are my ideas so alienating?"

"Sometimes you do fall wide of the mark," Brenda responded with her usual candour, "but ..."

"Yes?"

"Often you write with such elegance and power. Don't worry. Something positive will come of your efforts."

Sure enough, he did meet with some public acclaim. Perhaps this change had something to do with the fact that the war was finally over. Hostilities in Europe had ceased with Germany's capitulation on VE Day (May 8, 1945) — their surrender had been engineered by the successful D-Day landing on June 6, 1944 and the subsequent rolling back of German forces in the east and west. The Japanese effort, too, was also brought to an end in mid-August 1945 when the U.S. dropped two nuclear bombs — one on Hiroshima (code-named "Little Boy") and a second on Nagasaki ("Fat Man"). One way or another, Davies began to hit his stride.

His first success was *Overlaid*, written in late 1945. It is a charming one-act piece that sets an elderly farmer's love of opera against his daughter's religious zeal. When the farmer receives word that a hefty sum of money has come his way, he fantasizes about travelling to New York City and blowing the windfall on an opera performance and a striptease show; his daughter, for her part, advises the money be spent on a family plot and headstone. Unable to withstand his daughter's pragmatic outlook, the farmer finally acquiesces to her demands.

Davies tried to get *Overlaid* performed as part of the CBC Radio *Stage* series, but the script was rejected. The following year, however, it was awarded first prize at the Ottawa Drama League's Workshop competition and was performed by a variety of amateur stage companies that, with the end of the war, had sprouted across Canada.

Eros at Breakfast was written in the fall of 1946 and earned Davies even greater kudos. Like *Overlaid*, it is a one-act play but is comic in tone and presents a highly original story: a certain Mr. P.S. — short for "Psyche" (soul) and "Soma" (body) — has fallen in love with a woman named Thora while eating breakfast, but this fact is communicated to the audience by means of a discourse between the happy lover's organs and faculties; that is, a representative from the Heart department, one from

Intelligence, and a third from the Solar Plexus. The following is a sample exchange between Aristophontes (head of Mr. P.S.'s intelligence), Chremes (head of his Solar Plexus), and Crito (Chremes' assistant):

> ARISTOPHONTES: I'm going! When you wish to apologize you can reach me in the usual way.

> CHREMES: Oh, sit down, Aristophontes! If we quarrel like this, Mr. P.S. will have trouble with breakfast.

> CRITO (listening to the phone): A report, sir: Mr. P.S. is having trouble with his breakfast. He is grumbling about the new breakfast food, as well. The fireman in the Epigastrium is hinting at heartburn.

> CHREMES: Really? It would be a shame if Mr. P.S. developed a dyspeptic tendency. Makes such a lot of extra work.

> ARISTOPHONTES: Then be careful what you say. When the Intelligence and the Solar Plexus are at outs, anything can happen. And with this Thora business in the offing, we can't afford to have any gratuitous trouble.

For the second time in as many years, Davies won first prize from the Ottawa Drama League with *Eros* in 1947 — just at the time that his third daughter, Rosamond, was born. This triumph led *Eros* to be performed by a multitude of small companies, and in 1948 Davies's publisher, Clarke, Irwin, agreed to publish a collection of Davies's plays, with *Eros* as the principal component. And the Dominion Drama Festival, the country's foremost drama competition, chose *Eros* as the Canadian submission to the Edinburgh Festival for 1949.

Even as he immersed himself in the theatre world, Davies did not neglect his Marchbanks series. Marchbanks had been such a hit over the last seven years that Clarke, Irwin agreed to publish a collection of his columns. This appeared in 1947, at roughly the same time as the birth of Rosamond, and was entitled *The Diary of Samuel Marchbanks*. It sold exceptionally well, to the point that a second volume followed two years later — *The Table Talk of Samuel Marchbanks*. Davies even received letters of thanks and appreciation from renowned poet E.J. Pratt and Canadian prime minister Mackenzie King. More ambitious than ever, he starting sketching out a series of other plays, but was brought to a halt when faced with an unexpected setback.

"Pink, I have something important to tell you. You know that chronic cough of mine?" he told Brenda in the summer of 1947, while she was nursing their baby daughter.

"Yes?"

"Well, I went to see a doctor and he performed a battery of tests. I'm afraid the news isn't good."

"What is it? Pneumonia?"

"Worse than that. He's pretty sure it's Hodgkin's disease, which is another name for cancer of the lymphatic system. He says it could be fatal."

"Oh Rob! What are we going to do?"

"He recommends intense radiation treatment. I'll be leaving for Toronto in a couple of days. Pink, I want you to know that I refuse, positively refuse, to allow this illness, whatever it is, to get the better of me. I have four mouths to feed and plays to write and, well, that's all there is to it. And let's not mention anything to anyone."

Weeks of intense and uncomfortable treatment followed. Davies's sessions of X-ray treatment took place in Toronto, and this meant he was apart from his family and had to endure his illness in solitude. True to his word, however, he did not let the disease drag him under: he was eventually pronounced cured and was allowed to return home. In retrospect, it has been speculated that his doctor had possibly misdiagnosed a case of mononucleosis for cancer.

Picking up where he had left off, Davies resumed his busy schedule and, by the summer of 1948, had completed a full-length play, *Fortune, My Foe*. Set in a Kingston hangar that has been modified into a cabaret/bar, the play's central character, Nicholas Hayward, is a disgruntled academic who, convinced Canada does not respect its scholars, is scheming to join a university south of the border. A famous European puppeteer, Franz Szabo, then enters the scene and, encouraged by Nicholas and his friends, displays his mastery of marionettes, only to be scorned by two modern educational experts. While this treatment of the masterly Szabo only strengthens Nicholas's contention that Canadians are deaf and blind to genius, he decides at play's end that, if people like him retreat from the country, genuine art will never take root in Canada. He concludes:

> Everybody says Canada is a hard country to govern, but nobody mentions that for some people it is also a hard country to live in. Still, if we all run away it will never be any better. So

> let the geniuses of easy virtue go southward; I
> know what they feel too well to blame them.
> But for some of us there is no choice; let Canada
> do what she will with us, we must stay.

While some reviewers found *Fortune* wooden and clichéd, it was picked up by a host of companies and performed across the country. Together with his other plays, *Fortune* established Davies's reputation as one of Canada's foremost playwrights of that era.

But more trouble dogged Davies. As *Fortune* was winning praise in various parts of Canada, he was advised that his mother was critically ill. After several recoveries from the brink of death, all of them necessitating frenzied trips to the hospital in Kingston, Florence finally succumbed to her illness in the final days of 1948. Davies was sitting by himself in an adjoining room on the night she passed away.

"Rob, you look white as a ghost," Brenda stated the morning after Florence's death.

"I had the most ghastly dream last night, Pink. I wouldn't even say it was dream; it was more a ... visitation."

"Describe it to me."

"It was late, just getting on four a.m. I was in that mental state between wakefulness and sleep when suddenly a ghostly presence attacked me. She was female and dishevelled and full of rage and murderous intent. She went for my throat, in fact, and kept screaming, "Why couldn't you be closer to me?""

"Wait. I don't understand ..."

"I had to gather all my strength to ward her off. And if I hadn't won this wrestling match, she would have killed me, I'm sure of it. And when I awoke, and checked in on my mother, she was dead. Her limbs were still warm, and that meant she must have died just moments earlier."

"Rob, what are you saying?"

"It's obvious, isn't it? In her final, waking moments, my mother wanted to kill me. And before her soul could fly off to the netherworld, it staged a final attack on my person."

"You're overwrought, that's all. You're upset your mother's dead ..."

"That's not it at all, believe me. I disappointed her all along — she wanted me to be a pharmacist — and she used her last moments to express her hostility to me. My flesh is still crawling at the thought of this encounter."

"Your best bet is to forget this. Return to your plays and your nerves will settle down."

His mother's demise, and his own close brush with death, had provided Davies with an objective view of his record in the theatre world. Despite some genuine accomplishments, he understood the laurels he had won thus far were very small potatoes. To be a true playwright, he had to blaze a trail to Broadway or, more to his liking, the London stage. By late 1949, however, it was obvious England had no interest in his dramatic vision. *Eros at Breakfast* had been performed at the Edinburgh Festival and had failed to attract any significant notice. One English director told him in a moment of candour that Canada was off the map as far as British audiences were concerned.

Perhaps the problem was the very one he had diagnosed in most of his plays: Canada was still a cultural wilderness and, with his own developed literary sensitivities, he was sorely out of place in such an environment. He was Queen Emma who had to escape from Aethelred, or the elderly farmer in *Overlaid* who was being driven to distraction by his practical daughter, or

Franz Szabo whose subtle ways with puppets were wasted on the Canadian want of imagination.

One way or another, the lesson was clear: if his plays would not win him the fame he desired, he would have to steer his literary efforts in a different direction.

5

The Salterton Trilogy

Are there comic themes, or only comic writers
— men whose quality of mind and means of
expression are comic, without thereby being
any less compassionate or understanding or
profound than the writers of tragedy?
(*A Voice from the Attic*)

Nobody but a fool wants to fail when he sets to
work to write a novel, and it is the hope that he
may succeed where others — in so many ways
his better — have failed that keeps him going.
(*A Voice from the Attic*)

Never be deceived by a humorist, for if he is any
good he is a deeply serious man, moved by a

Robertson and Brenda Davies with members of the original cast of Fortune, My Foe, *1948. William Needles (Szabo) leaning on bar, Drew Thompson (Hayward) and Glenn Burns (Rowlands) are seated.*

quirk of temperament to speak a certain kind of
truth in the form of jokes. Everybody can laugh
at the jokes; the real trick is to understand them.
(*One Half of Robertson Davies*)

"I must say, Maimas, your methods take my breath away."

"Thank you, Zadkiel. It's not often anyone compliments me on my efforts."

"I'm hardly complimenting you, old boy. Quite the opposite, in fact. I mean, I understand why you steered Robertson into the newspaper business — this helped him with his real calling down the road. But that misdiagnosis mystifies me. Poor Robertson must have been tortured with worry when he thought his body was ravaged with cancer."

"It's all a matter of perspective, my dear fellow. Put yourself in Davies' shoes. Through no fault of his own — I'm referring to his poor eyesight now — he missed out on the struggle of his generation. That is, he didn't do his bit by fighting the Nazis. Imagine how this would have eaten at him while the troops returned from overseas. By frightening him with Hodgkin's disease, I gave him a sample taste of death."

"And that episode with his mother, when he wrestled with her spirit?"

"He's always had acute problems with Florence. If I hadn't arranged that wrestling match and forced him to stick up for himself against her, with his bare knuckles no less, this open wound would have festered before long and stood in the way of his creative talents."

"On the subject of his creative talent, the type he's known for, when does it surface?"

"Patience, Zadkiel, patience. I will get to it in its proper time."

In the early 1950s, Canada was enjoying an economic boom. The Second World War had ended five years earlier and, as one of the few Western powers whose industrial infrastructure was still intact, the country was able to become an exporting power. The population was rapidly growing because of a "baby boom" and increased immigration. And the government was no longer spending its revenues on fighting a war, and that meant money could be diverted to a range of domestic incentives.

It is true that a new Cold War had started between the Americans and the Soviets. As Winston Churchill expressed it at the time, "From Stettin in the Baltic to Trieste in the Adriatic an iron curtain has descended across the continent." Canada contributed generously to the American-led Western alliance. And when the Korean War erupted, as a result of the communist North's invasion of the democratic South, a Western coalition of forces was drawn into the melee, including Canadian troops. This exchange of hostilities, however, involved far fewer soldiers than the Second World War. After two years of fighting, Canada suffered fifteen hundred casualties, out of a contribution of some 27,000 troops. Overall, Canada was at peace, and as a whole the nation was very well-off.

Davies, too, was thriving. His domestic life was very stable — he and Brenda were admirably suited to each other and their three daughters were profiting from the benefits of a wealthy, well-structured, creative household. Davies was still editing the *Peterborough Examiner*, whose circulation had jumped from approximately nine thousand to sixteen thousand over a ten-year period — a record that so impressed several competing publishers that they tried to woo him over to their papers. (Rupert would hear of no such thing.) His two Marchbanks volumes enjoyed respectable sales, and his plays had rendered him the leading voice on the Canadian stage.

His reputation as a dramatist was so firmly entrenched that in the spring of 1950 he was approached to contribute a memorandum to the Massey Commission — a Royal Commission chaired by Vincent Massey (former High Commissioner to England). The purpose of the commission was to inquire into the state of the arts and sciences in Canada. Because of his experience with the Canadian theatre scene, Davies was asked to describe the condition of the dramatic arts and advance suggestions for their improvement down the road. As a result of his proposals, and those of other contributors, not only would the Canada Council program for funding of the arts take shape in the late 1950s but, more immediately, the Stratford Festival was created — an annual offering of first-rate theatrical productions involving world-class directors and performers.

For all these impressive achievements, however, Davies felt he had not yet left his mark and was intent on pushing his creative efforts further — with a twist, as it turned out.

"I have another idea for a play," he announced to Brenda, while the two of them were picnicking in the Ontario countryside.

"Oh. Tell me about it."

"I'd rather keep that secret for now. I'm just wondering what I'm going to do when the script is finished and ready to go."

"What do you mean?"

"I'm talking about the staging of the play, how I'll never persuade the companies I work with to respect my vision. As has happened several times now, the director, the actors, and the lighting and staging crew will use my story to further their own purposes."

"If you're so worried, why don't you cut these meddlers out of the equation?"

"That sounds wonderful, but I don't follow you, Pink."

"Instead of writing a play, why not write a novel? That way you won't have to relinquish control. The characters will act according to your will, and you'll control the setting, the costumes, the lighting, and everything else under the sun."

"You know, that's not a bad idea."

Curious to experiment with a new medium, Davies organized his story as a novel instead of a play, taking copious notes in the process. When he started on the actual writing, in September 1950, he discovered that he was adept at this narrative form and was able to work with breathtaking speed. As would be the case with all his novels, he typed a full, rough draft of the story, subjected the manuscript to handwritten revisions, had his secretary type the story again, then passed the new typescript through a second and final round of revisions. His grasp of language was so profound and his writing habits were so well-formed — although critics would later complain that his style bore a journalistic stamp — that his first rough draft did not differ much from the finished product. Indeed, once he had convinced his publisher Clarke, Irwin to take it on, it appeared on store bookshelves by October 1951.

Entitled *Tempest-Tost*, it is set in Salterton (the fictional name for Kingston) and describes the efforts of an amateur theatre group to stage an outdoor production of Shakespeare's *The Tempest*. The would-be players are a mix of middle-class characters, teachers, academics, and the children of property owners and businessmen, who for the most part are disgruntled with their secure circumstances, hence the attraction of acting in a play and escaping the tedium of their daily regimen.

Hector Mackilwraith best exemplifies this tortured outlook. In some ways the novel's central character, he is a well-respected instructor of mathematics who suffers from a singular lack of imagination and culture. Spying a notice for the play, he decides on impulse to join the proceedings and, at the very first meeting, falls head over heels in love with Griselda Webster, a young, careless socialite whose father's gardens are being used to host the production. Solly Bridgetower is Hector's rival for Griselda's affections. Recently returned from Cambridge and a junior professor at Salterton's Waverley College (a stand-in for Queen's University), Solly is appalled by the town's provincialism and, more to the point, longs to escape the suffocating control exerted by his aging, wealthy mother. Pearl Vambrace, the daughter of a local Classics professor, is in a similar bind: confined by her parents' narrow outlook (her mother's pull toward Catholicism and her father's pedantry and egotism) she is desperate to win some independence for herself, hence her attraction to Roger Tasset, a member of the local military college.

Once the stage has been set and his characters introduced, Davies chronicles the many difficulties, both logistical and psychological, that an amateur theatre production involves, and milks his story's love triangle to full effect. The novel's climax occurs when Hector realizes Griselda will never be his and, in a scene intended to be comic, sets about his suicide, only to fail when his hangman's noose snaps beneath his weight. Davies speculates (through his characters) that Hector's pathetic suicide attempt was the product of his removal from any type of belief, religious or artistic.

> "The way we see it, sir," said Tom [a gardener],...
> "is like this. Too many people today are like

this fellow Mackilwraith. They don't believe, and they haven't got the strength of mind to disbelieve. They won't get rid of religion, and they won't go after a religion that means anything. They just mess with religion. Now if this fellow Mackilwraith had been a believer ... he would have known that suicide is a sin, and his belief would have held him up in his trouble. And if he'd been an unbeliever he'd either have had too much guts to do it, or guts enough to finish it off proper. See?"

True love cannot flourish when the spirit is threadbare — this would be a conviction that Davies would adhere to for the length of his life. And no doubt this contention explains why the only characters who know true satisfaction in the novel are Valentine Rich, a talented theatre director who has returned to Salterton to settle her late grandfather's affairs, and Humphrey Cobbler, the local organist and Bohemian choir director.

Like many authors, Davies mined his own experiences when writing the novel and peopled it with characters whose attributes were derived from his friends and many acquaintances. The central story, the staging of a Shakespeare drama, paralleled Davies's experience with various amateur theatrical groups (and his involvement in *A Midsummer Night's Dream* back in England), while the setting for the play, Mr. Webster's manicured grounds, was based on Rupert's Kingston estate Calderwood. Griselda Webster, who refuses to commit herself to any one admirer, shared many elements in common with Davies's old flame Eleanor Sweezey. Humphrey Cobbler mirrored Davies's eccentric piano teacher from Renfrew, Percival

Kirby, and Hector Mackilwraith — the competent, humour-less math instructor — was an obvious literary double for Mr. Mackenzie — Davies's hated math teacher at Upper Canada College. Finally, Solly Bridgetower's efforts to put his days at Cambridge behind him and re-immerse himself in small-town Canadian life were drawn from Davies's personal evolution, as was the same character's struggle to liberate himself from a manipulative and domineering mother.

"Your novel's doing well," Mr. Clarke informed Davies over lunch at a Toronto club. "True enough, the *Globe and Mail* didn't like it much, but the *Toronto Daily Star* and *Saturday Night* have both been very complimentary. Chatto and Windus, too, will be bringing out an English edition, while Rinehart will publish it in the States. Not bad. Not bad at all."

"I'm glad to hear it."

"More to the point, the reading public loves it. They always respond well to something that makes them laugh. It must be flattering to discover you're funny."

"To tell you the truth, I don't think I'm funny at all. A more accurate word would be comical."

"It's six of one, half a dozen of the other."

"Not quite. When you're funny, you make people laugh by any means available — by having someone slip on a banana peel, for example. Comedy, on the other hand, stirs laughter by revealing paradoxical and contradictory elements in the human condition. When we strive to be serious, we make fools of ourselves. When we set out to achieve certain grand ambitions, we end up falling flat on our faces."

"You seem to be saying comedy and tragedy are linked to each other."

"That's exactly what I'm saying. And the ancient Greeks

understood as much when they associated both forms of entertainment with the god Dionysus."

"Well, whether you're funny or comical, keep up the good work."

Davies was anxious to keep up the good work and was already taking notes for his second novel, a possible sequel to the first. There were two interruptions, however.

At the behest of Clarke, Irwin, he compiled yet another set of columns for a third volume in his Marchbanks series — it was entitled *Marchbanks' Almanack*. After Davies invested a great deal of labour in this project, however, Clarke, Irwin pulled the plug on it on the grounds Davies's humour was occasionally too low.

Greatly taken with Davies's obvious abilities, J.K. Cooke, the owner of *Saturday Night*, offered him substantial money to return as literary editor. Although Davies's plate was already full, what with his work for the *Examiner*, his success as a novelist, and his enduring ambition to write for the theatre, he could not bring himself to turn this offer down and started working for Cooke in January 1953. He would continue with this position until March 1959.

The position required him to read voluminously on a wide array of subjects. At any given moment he might be required to review a book on the corset, magic, Christmas, plumbing, music, art criticism, and a huge number of other eclectic subjects. At the same time he reviewed books by dozens of writers, both old and modern: Joyce Cary, Nabokov, Hemingway, Thomas Mann, Thomas Hardy, Chaucer, the list rolled on and on. The job clearly required someone whose experience of the Western canon was sufficiently profound to place new writings within a historical context and comment meaningfully on their relative strengths and weaknesses. It also demanded of the editor sound reading habits, which Davies himself described in an imagined dialogue he wrote for *Saturday Night*, entitled "A Chat with a Great Reader":

> MYSELF: You don't do enough for the books you read.
>
> THE MAN: Explain.
>
> MYSELF: Well, I think you should be ready to give as much effort to reading as you do to listening to music, or watching a play. You ought to be alert to every shade of meaning, and you ought to give the book a good mental performance, if I make myself clear.
>
> THE MAN: You don't.
>
> MYSELF: When Emlyn Williams [a well-known actor and playwright] visited Canada, reading the works of Dickens, did you hear him?
>
> THE MAN: I went to hear him four times, and I'd have gone again if it had been possible.
>
> MYSELF: ... When you read books yourself, you ought to read them like Williams ... You ought to give them all that fire and concentration. You ought to bring all that imagination to them, all that rhetoric and histrionic skill, or you are not being fair to your author.

Did Davies himself follow this prescription? Here is an excerpt from his review of Aldous Huxley's *Doors of Perception*, a work in which the famous author documents his experiments with LSD, under a scientist's strict supervision:

"Personality" means simply the externals of Self, and for many people Self has little existence apart from "personality." But there have always been people [like Huxley] who knew that "personality" was a shell, and that Self in the deeper sense was the reality which was capable, in its turn, of participation in the non-Self — which is God, or the Clear Light of the Void, or whatever you choose to call it.... If I am not mistaken, Huxley's later work has been a plea to mankind to recognize the perishability, and the essential triviality, of all the externals of daily life and of "personality"; and the infinite preciousness and imperishability of that essential Self which yearns to be united with the non-Self.

The clarity of expression, deep contextual knowledge, and scrupulous impartiality that Davies brought to this particular review were characteristic of his efforts in general. *Saturday Night* was lucky to have him on board.

The one drawback to Davies's Herculean labours was that he was too distracted to spend much time with his three daughters. He was prone to fits of temper, moreover, when the children proved too noisy or interrupted his work. Brenda was the one who kept the household running, and if the children had any pressing demands, they would approach her first.

"Dad! You're not listening!" Jennifer complained as the family sat around the dinner table — just the four of them because Brenda was off visiting her family in Australia.

"I am, in fact, listening. You were telling me, in ungrammatical English, that when the time comes for you to attend Bishop

Strachan in Toronto, an illustrious school that will make a lady out of you, you will run away and join the circus."

"I didn't say anything about the circus! I said I wanted to stay here at home and I wished you and Mom wouldn't travel so much."

"But if you were to run away and join the circus, what type of job would you perform for them? Would you be a sword swallower, the wild woman of Borneo, the obese lady, or the bearded female wonder?"

"You're still not listening. I wish Mom was here."

"You mean, you wish your mother *were* here."

Davies finally began working in earnest on his second novel, *Leaven of Malice*. Possibly he contrived it as a sequel to *Tempest-Tost* straight from the beginning, or it gradually developed into one as it was being assembled. One way or another, its setting was Salterton and its main characters were carried over from his previous novel.

The novel opens with the following notice that appears in Salterton's paper, the *Evening Bellman*:

> Professor and Mrs. Walter Vambrace are pleased to announce the engagement of their daughter, Pearl Veronica, to Solomon Bridgetower, Esq., son of Mrs. Bridgetower and the late Professor Solomon Bridgetower of this city. Marriage to take place in St. Nicholas' Cathedral at eleven o'clock a.m., November 31st.

The problem is, the news is false and creates much embarrassment for the parties involved. While Pearl and Solly would sooner forget the matter, Pearl's father, Professor Walter Vambrace, who carries a grudge against Solly's deceased father, is convinced his family's honour has been besmirched and launches a lawsuit against the *Evening Bellman*, despite the apologies he has received from its sympathetic editor, Gloster Ridley. Solly and Pearl strive to untangle the misunderstanding, but the more they attempt to extricate themselves from one another, the more entwined they become. As in *Tempest-Tost*, both are chained to their parent's will, but while Solly suffers his servitude in silence, Pearl is finally pushed to gain her independence when her father spies her emerging from Solly's car, concludes she has behaved indecently, and handles her with surprising roughness. Pearl's reaction is described pointedly and with remarkable power:

> Pearl was still weeping, but silently, when dawn
> came through her window. She felt herself to
> be utterly alone and forsaken, for she knew that
> she had lost her father, more certainly than if he
> had died that night.

Walter Vambrace is further discredited when, in Gloster Ridley's office, he attributes the false announcement to Humphrey Cobbler, the local organist, only to be shown concrete proof that one Bevill Higgin, an Irish con artist, was the actual culprit. Happily, even as this process of discovery has unfolded, Pearl and Solly have learned they have a great deal in common with each other and are, in fact, in love, and the novel ends with the following genuine announcement:

> Professor and Mrs. Walter Vambrace are pleased
> to announce the engagement of their daughter,

Pearl Veronica, to Solomon Bridgetower, Esq.,
son of Mrs. Bridgetower and the late Professor
Solomon Bridgetower of this city. Marriage to
take place in St. Nicholas' Cathedral at a date to
be announced later.

Just as he was setting the finishing touches on *Leaven of Malice*, Davies received unpleasant news in March 1954: his oldest brother Fred had died in a car crash in Nassau. In contrast to his brothers, Fred had not played his cards very well and had been through a particularly difficult stage in recent years. His desperation, together with the fact that he had been a very skilled driver, led his relatives to suppose that his death had been deliberate on his part. And while Davies and Fred had never been close — two years prior to the accident the pair had argued violently when visiting Rupert in Wales — the news still came as a dreadful blow.

"I've finally finished reading the last draft of your novel," Brenda announced, to distract her husband from his brother's death. It had been a month since the accident and it was only now that Davies had managed to complete *Leaven of Malice*.

"I'm glad to hear it. Do you like it?"

"It's a comedy of manners, isn't it?"

"It is, but what do you mean by that description?"

"You set society's values, as expressed by busybodies who champion the public good, in opposition to your heroes' individual will."

"Top of the class."

"And I think your point is a valid one, that it takes a wise man to understand that a disruptive situation can have a beneficial aspect."

"So, you like the book?"

"Some characters come off meanly, though. You don't understand the working class at all."

"So the book is a failure?"

"But the Freudian elements are dark and delicious — the children's tension with their overbearing parents. You handle that theme with insight and sensitivity, probably because the subject is so close to you."

"So, it sounds like you think the book is a success."

"Listen to you! The book is the best thing you've written yet."

Brenda's remark about the Freudian elements in *Leaven of Malice*, while correct, was at the same time ironic. Since his sessions with Dr. Gillespie years before in England, Davies had been an avid student of Freud; yet it was at this juncture that he started questioning his dedication to the psychoanalytic perspective. There were many aspects of Freud's arguments that bothered him, but the most egregious one was the master's lack of patience with anything religious. Such indifference worried Davies immensely as his own view of religion was considerably less dismissive.

As a boy he had attended a Presbyterian church whose depiction of God as a kind and gentle soul (through the figure of Jesus) had disgusted him: his own view of God emphasized the power that He wielded, with utter, frightening implacability. Later on in life, after his initial, trying year at Oxford, Davies had also come to reject the Presbyterian insistence on Predestination — the belief that God has foreordained eternal life for a select few, even before humans have been born into the world — and savoured instead the beauty of the Anglican prayers and service. Having received formal instruction in Anglicanism, he had finally decided to join this church and leave his parents' gloomy, Calvinist principles behind.

Even within the context of traditional religious observance, however, Davies's understanding of religion had always remained broad-minded and complex.

"What do you mean by 'religion'?" his oldest daughter asked him as she was being driven back to her private school in Toronto.

"That's a good question," her father answered, glad to be distracted from the pain of having to part with his daughter. "There are at least two popular derivations. One comes from the Latin verb *religare* — and that's a nice part about the school you're attending, they'll instruct you in Latin — and this word means 'to fasten' or 'to assume a yoke.'"

"So that means religion yokes us to something?"

"Yes, something like that. People who accept this derivation believe religion binds us to certain traditions and rules."

"You're not all that crazy about rules."

"Some rules yes, and some rules no. And that's why I'm attracted to the second derivation, from the Latin verb *relegere*, which means 'to ponder,' 'to examine,' and literally 'to reread.' Under this interpretation, religion forces us to examine the world closely and not be fooled by superficial appearances. Beneath the surface of things lurks the fires of the real world, and our job is to apprehend them."

"You mean the way beneath your beard and fancy dress is the *real* Robertson Davies?"

"That's a perfect example."

Put off, then, by Freud's dismissal of his religious instincts, as well as other broad features of psychoanalysis, Davies turned to the writings of Carl Jung, who had started as a student of Freud's but had come to disagree with fundamental aspects of his theories. Whereas Freud was Jewish and a city dweller, Jung was Christian and had grown up in the country (like Davies): in other words, his basic experiences and outlook paralleled Davies's own.

More to the point, Jung eschewed Freud's obsession with sex as a primary element in human behaviour, as well as his theory that the human unconscious was essentially a storehouse of repressed emotions. He instead proposed that the human psyche could be best understood not only through a study of dreams (as Freud had suggested) but through world religion, mythology, art, and philosophy. Religion and mythology could reveal a great deal about humans because, according to Jung, human souls not only had a personal unconscious — this consisted of thoughts and memories that are not immediately before us — but a collective unconscious (or collective psyche) as well. This aspect of the soul was universal and contained the species' collective experiences that arose spontaneously in the individual's mind as part of our genetic inheritance. The key component of the collective unconscious was the "archetypes" — religious and spiritual emotions and experiences that were common to all societies, past and present. Examples of such archetypes (which were practically limitless) would be the Wise Old Man, the Great Mother, the Hero, the Trickster, the Eternal Youth, and other such figures that, according to Jung, recurred repeatedly in all mythologies and literatures. This last point was a telling one: mythology, art, literature, and even religion were of profound importance for self-understanding because they manifested the archetypes, and therefore the hidden reality, underpinning our humanity.

Even as Davies studied Jung's interpretation of spirit at the expense of his former allegiance to Freud, he worked simultaneously on the third of his Salterton novels and a new play, *Hunting Stuart*. The latter tells the story of a minor civil servant, Henry Stuart, whom scientists believe is a descendant of the Stuart kings; they set about proving this by exposing Henry to a special powder that triggers his "ancestral memory" — a Jungian idea. This play enjoyed a good two-week run in Toronto, then petered out.

The last tale in the Salterton Trilogy, *A Mixture of Frailties*, proved a greater success. The novel opens with the funeral of Mrs. Bridgetower and the reading of her will. Her son Solly feels the "dead hand" of his mother when he learns that her estate (and his rightful inheritance) is to be used to promote the musical education of a local girl until he and his wife, Pearl Vambrace, can produce a son between them. The "hick" Monica Gall is the lucky recipient of this legacy, and the novel then traces her departure for England and her extensive musical training at the hands of several experts. The magisterial Sir Benedict Domdaniel, a world-renowned conductor, teaches Monica that a dedicated application of one's talent can lead to self-knowledge and a life free of illusion. Giles Revelstoke, a brilliant composer, pushes Monica to abandon the normal conventions — he has an affair with her — and to extend her range of feeling. When she questions her attempts to become a singer, Revelstoke explains to her the purpose of the artist:

> Poetry and music can speak directly to depths of experience within us which we possess without being conscious of them, in language which we understand only imperfectly. But there must be some of us who understand better than others, and who give the best of ourselves to that understanding. If you are to

be one of them, you must be ready to make a painful exploration.

Unfortunately, Revelstoke's creative powers are accompanied by a destructive egoism and, dissatisfied with the reaction to his opera *The Golden Ass*, he turns to suicide. The novel ends on a happy note, however, when Domdaniel, having lifted Monica to his own artistic standards, seeks to take her as his wife. Solly and Pearl manage to produce a son, thereby regaining his mother's estate for themselves, although (in a macabre twist) Pearl must protect her newborn child from the onslaught of her mother-in-law's ghost — a clear reference to Davies's own struggle with his departing mother's soul.

"Bob?" someone asked in a late night call two weeks before *A Mixture of Frailties* was scheduled for release.

"Who is this?"

"It's me, Arnold Edinborough, your colleague at *Saturday Night*. Did I wake you up?"

"It's one a.m. Of course you woke me up."

"Sorry. I couldn't contain myself. I've just finished *A Mixture of Frailties*, and I have to say you've surpassed yourself. You've described an artist's apprenticeship convincingly, and left your usual comic twists behind for something more sobering and serious."

"Speak up, would you? I can barely hear you."

"You'll receive some flak because Monica has premarital sex, and you treat her people with unnecessary disdain, but these are minor quibbles. All in all you do justice to the transcendent nature of art."

"That's all very nice, but can I go back to bed?"

On his completion of *A Mixture of Frailties*, Davies was forty-five years old. While his Salterton Trilogy had posted respectable sales, at Davies's age many artists would have put their most creative years behind them. And with all the energy Davies had exerted, on his plays and journalism in addition to his novels, a critic would have been excused for concluding that Davies was an aging, worn-out Canadian writer who had little that was original to contribute to the literary scene. Davies himself was brought to doubt this assessment when, on the advice of a friend, he visited a famous astrologer in New York City in December 1958.

"You're not serious," Brenda scolded him. "You travelled to New York to consult with an astrologer? I can't believe you'd put faith in such hocus-pocus."

"For your information, Jung argues that astrology, when meaningfully practised, can reveal certain truths about the human condition. I decided to take him up on this suggestion."

"There are plenty of fortune tellers whom you could have consulted with here in Toronto."

"But they aren't bona fide. This Hugh McCraig, who comes highly recommended, has studied the science as it was practised in medieval times. As Jung points out, a craft so old and venerable must embody its fair share of psychological insight."

"So what did Mr. Con Artist tell you?"

"He said I'm highly intuitive and more a metaphysical, spiritual type than a scientific one."

"It sounds like he read your report card from Grade Five."

"He also said I'm entering a crucial stage in my career that will last for several decades."

"Do these people ever have anything negative to say?"

"He spoke about you, too. He said you're an old soul and something of an instructor. He suggested that I listen closely to your advice."

"Why didn't you say so from the beginning? He sounds like a wise old dear!"

Hocus-pocus or not, time would prove that this reading of Davies's future was remarkably prescient.

6

Massey College

Universities were creations of the Middle Ages, and much of the Middle Ages still clings to them, not only in their gowns and official trappings, but deep in their hearts.
(*The Rebel Angels*)

To instruct calls for energy, and to remain almost silent, but watchful and helpful, while students instruct themselves, calls for even greater energy. To see someone fall (which will teach him not to fall again) when a word from you would keep him on his feet but ignorant of an important danger, is one of the tasks of the

Leaving Hart House on the way to the ceremonial laying of the cornerstone of Massey College. May 25, 1962. Dr. F.C.A. Jeanneret, chancellor of the university, Davies, and Dr. Claude Bissell, president of the university leading off. Photo by Jack Marshall Ltd.

teacher that calls for special energy, because holding in is more demanding than crying out.
(*The Rebel Angels*)

Academicism runs in the blood like syphilis.
(*The Rebel Angels*)

"Now that's more like it, Maimas. Instead of tormenting Robertson, you've finally created a proper state of affairs. He's prosperous, well-respected, successful, and —"

"No, no, no! You have it all wrong, Zadkiel."

"Steady on, all man. There's no need to become so hot under the collar. I was only saying —"

"If Robertson had written nothing else for the rest of his career, other than his plays and Salterton Trilogy, do you know what he would amount to?"

"Another figure in the Canadian pantheon of writers, I presume."

"Yes, precisely. Another meandering, complacent writer, who shot his bolt, hit a couple of rabbits, and retreated to his subterranean cave with the spoils. I expected more of him. Why else do you think I inspired that New York astrologer and prompted him to tell Robertson that his best years were ahead of him? I wasn't expecting mere self-satisfied competence from him; I was aiming for nothing less than greatness, with all the uncertainty and insomnia and self-torture true artistry involves."

"So, the poor soul has plenty of knocks ahead of him still?"

"What doesn't kill us strengthens us, as another charge of mine once wrote."

In seeming contrast to Hugh McCraig's flattering predictions, the new decade began with a terrible setback for Davies. As early as 1956, producers in New York had invited Davies to write a play based on his Salterton novel, *Leaven of Malice.* Over the next three years, Davies had written a couple of outlines, but these had proven second-rate. On the advice of a producer with New York City's Theater Guild, Davies wrote a new script and flew to Ireland to work with Tyrone Guthrie, his one-time boss at the Old Vic Theatre. Incorporating some of his mentor's suggestions, Davies came up with another script that Guthrie in turn agreed to produce. The title of the play was now *Love and Libel.*

After extensive rehearsals, *Love and Libel* opened in Toronto in October 1960. The reviews were mixed. It was then taken on tour to several American cities, including Detroit and Boston, but again the audiences' responses were lukewarm. When the play finally arrived in New York City, it closed after a mere five performances. Davies was devastated and thought this debacle meant the end of his literary career.

"You can't win them all," Guthrie announced as three workers cleared a large double bed from the stage.

"I would like to win just one," Davies answered, through half-clenched teeth.

"You have to look to the future and not dwell on the present."

"That's easy for you to say. You have other plays to direct."

"Look, Bob, the theatre's a rough place. It makes the boxing ring look like a child's sandbox. If you can't roll with the punches, you shouldn't enter the lists."

As Davies continued to gnaw on his frustration, an unusual offer arrived from out of the blue a couple of weeks after his play's flop in New York City. Vincent Massey, one-time High

Commissioner to England and Governor General of Canada from 1952 to 1959, was intent on using part of his family fortune to create a new college in the heart of Toronto. This institution would serve as a residence for male graduate students and recreate the atmosphere of Balliol and other Oxbridge colleges, instilling in its members a desire to toil for the public good. It would be populated by a mix of resident and non-resident Junior Fellows — M.A. and Ph.D. students from the University of Toronto — and by visiting academics, dubbed "senior fellows," from a range of disciplines. A smattering of journalists, too, on a year's leave from their papers, would complement these full-time students and scholars. Finally, the new college would be affiliated with, but strictly independent of, the University of Toronto.

Such an institution would require a master, but one who could bring unique skills to the college. On the one hand there were the job's practical dimensions: hiring staff members, recruiting senior fellows, managing a budget, organizing talks and social events, and ensuring that the college, on a daily basis, adhered to its primary educational mandate. At the same time an able master, in Massey's opinion, would expose students to the civilizing influence of the arts and afford them a wider prospective of world events and public affairs.

"But why me?" Davies asked Vincent Massey at Batterwood, the latter's country estate. "Surely you could find other people for the job. After all, I'm not an academic."

"But don't you see? I'm not looking for an academic. Academics are a dime a dozen here within the university. I'm looking for a figure who can draw the civilizing elements together — vast knowledge, the spirit of inquiry, and, I dare say, a certain playfulness."

"My critics will tell you that I never graduated from high school and attained a mere B.Litt. at Oxford — a second-rate degree."

"I think I'm able to look beyond the superficiality of mere papered credentials. You are an expert on Victorian drama. You have run a newspaper for close to twenty years, have written numerous plays, have penned three delightful novels, have produced a scholarly work on Shakespeare, and digested more books, I warrant, than several academics combined. No, my mind is made up. You are the just the ticket for Massey College."

"You will have difficulty persuading the committee that I am as attractive as you think."

"We already have Northrop Frye on our side — as Canada's leading academic I suspect he can defuse a great deal of the fuss you'll encounter. And Marshall McLuhan approves as well — he'll get the message across, media or otherwise."

"I'll have to move away from Peterborough ..."

"Don't be such a fox! You're dying to leave Peterborough for the bright lights of Toronto. But enough is enough. You will be the first master of Massey College and that's all there is to it. Now, how about a little champagne before dinner?"

Massey was right. Davies was bent on accepting the position, although he did consult with Brenda and his father first. The former was taken with the prospect of returning to Toronto; the latter advised his son that the opportunity was golden and couldn't be turned down. Davies's daughters had their doubts — they felt the eyes of the college would be focussed on them, and their father kept warning them that they would have to do him credit — but they were entering their adult years and would soon be independent of their parents' will.

When Massey College finally opened and received its first students in 1963, Davies was determined to create an atmosphere of tradition and collegiality. Besides building up the library and ensuring the decor and accoutrements were tasteful, he devoted himself to the creation of occasions on which residents from the various disciplines would gather together and inspire each other. With help from his colleagues, he organized a series of dinners that were attended by prominent guests, academics, journalists, politicians, and artistic figures. These formal meals were modelled on the "high tables" at Oxford, as were the college's croquet tournaments, the wearing of gowns, and the insistence on "gentlemanly behaviour" with one's peers and the staff. Davies also instituted Tuesday night buffets as a means of bringing the fellows together and encouraging experts from different disciplines to mingle. There were also cocktail parties that allowed the male student body to invite in female students from the surrounding university. And finally, there was Gaudy night.

Held at Christmastime, the Gaudy featured dramatic and musical presentations from a range of talented people. The Massey College Singers would perform Christmas choral music, local composers could launch their latest compositions, and poets would recite their newest creations. The crowning event of the evening, however, was Davies's contribution: his annual ghost story. Set in the college and featuring Davies himself — in one he appeared as a ghost — these became a favourite ritual with the student body.

Not that Davies's tenure at the college was all fun and games. As master he was expected to lecture within the university, and therefore each year he taught undergraduate courses on English drama, his own field of expertise. Although he had been praised for his speaking abilities in the past, he received very mixed reviews as an instructor, possibly because he played favourites with his students and was occasionally gruff with them.

"When we confront plays from the Victorian period," Davies declaimed before a small group of students in his course English

Drama from 1800 to the Present, "and I'm not referring to the masters of this period, but to playwrights who were popular then and are nonentities in our own day and age — figures such as Lytton, Planché, and Henry Arthur Jones — the question that intrigues me is why these plays struck such a chord back then yet have lost their power in the intervening decades ..."

"He does go on," one student whispered to his neighbour.

"Shh, I'm listening," she replied.

"... This question leads us to a prime consideration of this course. By this I mean the electrifying qualities that a brilliant actor can bring to the dullest of texts, or how staging and music can transform a middling play into first-rate theatre that leaves viewers hanging on the edge of their seats ..."

"How much longer till the end of class?" the same man whispered. "We can go and get a drink afterward."

"All right, but let me listen."

"... Although the point is obvious, it bears repetition. When we encounter plays in a lecture-hall setting, we see them as mere words on paper. You must always keep in mind that these words, in the eyes of the playwright himself, are only part of the overall theatrical equation, to be filled out by the director, the staging, and the actors' interpretation. A play, in other words, is like a musical score. The notes mean little until the conductor and musicians bring them to life. Are there any questions? You there, Mr. Johnson."

"Yes, professor?"

"No doubt you have something profound to contribute, as I notice you've been talking non-stop to your neighbour."

"Uh, no sir. I've just been drinking your lecture in."

"I suspect you'd rather be drinking something else. Anyone else, then? No? Nothing at all? God, you're a dull lot, aren't you?"

Part of Davies's problem was that the times were changing. The children born in the wake of the Second World War had come of age and were impatient with the conservatism, formality, and materialism of their parents' generation. Exasperated with the Cold War stalemate between the U.S. and the Soviet Union, especially with its latest manifestation, a burgeoning war in Vietnam, and exhilarated by the Civil Rights Movement that was finally granting rights and dignity to the American Black population, "baby-boomers" were prepared to turn the accepted conventions upside down, creating a widespread counterculture. Change, often violent, would become the hallmark of the decade — this was the era that witnessed widespread rioting across the States, endless demonstrations, and political assassinations (John F. Kennedy, Robert Kennedy, Martin Luther King, Malcolm X).

In Canada, legions of young people would greet the arrival of Pierre Trudeau on the political scene with unprecedented enthusiasm. Young, dynamic, and imbued with the spirit of the times, Trudeau would launch far-reaching political reforms through his tenure as prime minister.

The effects of the decade on daily life were immediate. A new music burst upon the scene: the airwaves were dominated by performers like The Beatles, The Rolling Stones, Bob Dylan, and the Motown sound. With the wide availability of the birth control pill, the Sexual Revolution came alive, and a new urgent public dialogue on women's rights appeared on the political landscape. Censorship laws were softened, dress codes were relaxed, drug use was widespread and, overall, traditional Western norms were repeatedly assailed, especially on university campuses.

Massey College was not immune to these changes. Thinking the college's practices were artificial and out-of-date, students questioned the gowns, the curfews, and the absence of a female student body. Some protesters wanted to inspect the college's funding and have some say in how this money was disbursed; they also wanted to form committees that would challenge the board and represent student demands. As far as the master himself was concerned, while they appreciated his efforts on their behalf, they objected to his formal bearing, his projection of elitism, and his refusal to admit women into the college.

To a great degree, Davies was guilty as charged. Since his days at North Ward School in Renfrew, and his encounter with the unkempt, bullying sons of the local farmers, he had developed a visceral distrust of the "common man." His later development only fortified his early prejudice. His experiences at Upper Canada College, Canada's foremost private school, his three-year tenure at Oxford with its air of exclusivity, his enjoyment of wealth as his father's career had advanced, and the influence the latter had exerted as a well-connected businessman and senator — these factors drove a wedge between Davies and the working population, heightening his suspicion of them and often stirring his contempt.

With his "upper-crust" upbringing, then, Davies refused to indulge people whom he thought to be his inferiors, and communicated this antipathy to his daughters, forbidding them to interact with "common" children. He also rejected the idea that the "common man" should intrude on university affairs or meddle in the arts. Indeed, it was Davies's "refinement" that had led Massey to consider him for the mastership to start with. With ironclad, patrician views of his own — he had supported, for example, Mackenzie King's bias against Jewish refugees during the Second World War — Massey represented the cream of the cream and, like Davies, rejected anything that had a "popular" air to it: Hollywood films, jazz and rock 'n roll, and most manifestations of American culture.

On the subject of women, Davies was far less consistent. Within the classroom he insisted that women, while more perceptive and intuitive than their male counterparts, were considerably less analytical and could never become genuine scholars. He also had very traditional views about the domestic roles of husband and wife: the husband was the lord and master who, because he provided for the family, was entitled to remove himself from the "female" tasks of cooking, cleaning, childrearing, and the like. At the same time, he respected Brenda deeply and encouraged her in all her acting projects, even as he was appreciative of her efforts to keep their household running smoothly. At the university, he promoted the careers of female scholars and unfailingly recognized their contributions to the college, even if he maintained his prohibition against female students.

Most tellingly, Davies's treatment of his female, fictional characters was always open-minded and full of surprises. These women were not only intelligent and forthright — characters like Pearl Vambrace, Valentine Rich, and Monica Gall — but were sexually daring and experimental in outlook ... characteristics that Davies would have preferred to ignore in his real-life dealings with the opposite sex, including his daughters, who were involved in serious relationships at this time.

"John and I have something important to tell you," Davies's youngest daughter Rosamond announced one February evening in 1968.

"Is it about that trip you mentioned? The one to Europe?"

"No sir," John spoke up. "As it turns out, Rosamond is pregnant. We plan to get married as soon as possible."

"You're ... pregnant?" Davies practically stuttered.

"Isn't it wonderful? We were thinking of a summer wedding ..."

"But you're not married! How could you?! What on earth are my colleagues at the college going to think?!"

It was at the height of the student unrest that another blow befell Davies: his father died at the age of 87. Despite some rough spots in his dealings with Davies — ones that would emerge down the road in a novel — Rupert had been an affectionate parent and his death had a severe impact on the family. At the same time, his affairs had to be put in order. As executor of his father's estate, Davies had to travel to Wales and dispense with Rupert's property and all its furnishing. One detail that made these activities particularly hard was that Rupert, not trusting his sons' business instincts, had bypassed them in his will and divided his wealth among his grandchildren. Years earlier, it was true, Rupert had ceded the *Peterborough Examiner* to his sons. They sold the paper in 1968 for $3.1 million, 30 percent of which fell into Davies's hands, freeing him from any future monetary concerns. Neither this fortune, however, nor the consideration that his children would be provided for through their grandfather's legacy, diminished his conviction that he had been personally passed over.

Despite his many responsibilities, Davies did enjoy some periods of freedom. The academic year afforded him plenty of time off, and his daughters now had lives of their own: Miranda had moved out by this time and was studying singing at the University of Toronto, Jennifer had married in 1966, and Rosamond followed suit in 1969, with her first child already in hand. Intent on taking full advantage of their liberty, Davies and Brenda started travelling extensively, not just to the British Isles but to the Continent as well. Over a period of several years the couple toured Italy, France, Germany, Austria, Portugal, and other countries, often renting a car that Brenda piloted across a host of foreign landscapes. On these journeys Davies developed a passion for statues of the Madonna and, over time, became something of an expert on them. On one trip to Austria in 1966, he and Brenda purchased a small Madonna standing on a globe and crescent moon. Greatly taken with this statuette, he could not guess how much of an inspiration it would prove when he started work on his next novel.

On this same trip he had a powerful experience. He and Brenda were staying in Kitzbuhel, Austria and had driven to Salzburg to attend an opera. It was late at night by the time the spectacle was over, and Brenda wanted to drive through part of Germany to return to their hotel, not daring to navigate the more difficult Austrian road at night. The problem was Davies had not brought his passport along and could not cross the German border, and every hotel in Salzburg was full. With no choice in the matter, the couple parked by the side of a country road and Brenda fell asleep in the back seat. Davies was too restless to settle down.

"Could my life have been any different?" he mused as he stared into the darkness and drank in the sounds of a nearby river. "And am I headed in the right direction?"

"You are exactly where you are supposed to be," he answered himself. "You have relied all your life on your intuition, and that has been an excellent choice because your personality is an intuitive one. Indeed, your life could have not have unfolded in any other fashion."

"But am I satisfied?" he wondered. Again, he stared into the darkness around him, then glanced towards the back seat where Brenda lay sleeping. His daughters, too, came briefly to mind.

"I am tremendously satisfied," he decided. "Never mind the drudgery I have endured at Massey College. Never mind the plays of mine that have never been produced. My life, thus far, has been a beautiful construct, has provided me with undeserved satisfaction, and, I dare say, has benefitted others."

"And the future?" he asked, wondering briefly what the surrounding shadows portended.

"It is bright," he decided. "In fact, I'm only getting started."

He needed to reassure himself. His efforts on behalf of Massey College had consumed so much of his time that he had been kept from pursuing any major writing projects. He had only written *A Masque for Mr. Punch* (1962) — a one-act play that was centred round the traditional Punch and Judy dramas, a subject that had long fascinated Davies. This effort had proven popular with high schools across Canada, to the point it had been published by Oxford University Press.

In an effort to jump-start his writing instincts, Davies wrote a play in celebration of Canada's hundredth anniversary in 1967 at the invitation of the Centennial Commission. The project came to nothing. He also collaborated with other prominent artists to produce a spectacle for the Ottawa centennial celebrations, but it too was cancelled.

Undaunted, he set about building a house in the Caledon area — a spacious, beautiful residence that he and Brenda would move into when Davies retired from Massey College. "Windhover," they decided to call it. And he finally published with McClelland and Stewart the third volume in his Marchbanks series, *Marchbanks' Almanack* (1967), which was subtitled *An Astrological and Inspirational* Vale Mecum *Containing Character Analyses, Secrets of Charm, Health Hints, How to be a Success at Parties, Fortune-Telling by the Disposition of Moles on the Body and Diverse Other Arcane Knowledge Here Revealed for the First Time; as Well as Generous Extracts from the Correspondence,* Pensées, *Musings,* Obiter Dicta *and Ruminations of Wizard Marchbanks.* While the book proved popular with readers, some critics found its humour forced and out of date.

He also wrote a book on Canadian humorist Stephen Leacock, although it was his contention that he preferred to *be* a Canadian writer rather than to write about one. His previous books, as well, were reissued in paperback and were therefore more accessible to the public. Although pleased with these successes, Davies felt he could do better. The question was how.

From out of the blue, Brenda provided him with a crucial piece to the puzzle.

"Did you have a good time at Goldschmidt's place?" he asked her late one evening as she entered their residence at Massey College.

"It was tremendous," she replied. "Someone was talking on and on about opera."

"God, that must have bored you. Some people have no sense of proportion."

"Actually, part of it was interesting. He said that the heroes of opera are performed by the sopranos and tenors, while the villains are performed by basses and contraltos."

"There's nothing new in that. Any halfwit could have made that observation."

"Perhaps. But then he spoke of certain singers whose sole purpose is to keep the plot rolling; without them, he said, the story would collapse. The term he used for these figures was one I hadn't heard before. He called them 'fifth business.'"

"Fifth business? Fifth business? What an interesting phrase."

Crucial elements were falling into place.

Detail from the Adoration of the Virgin *by Pietro Perugino, fifteenth century. Angels are a recurring theme in Davies's work.*

7

The Deptford Trilogy

He was a genius — that is to say, a man who does superlatively and without obvious effort something that most people cannot do by the uttermost exertion of their abilities.
(*Fifth Business*)

Every man has a devil, and a man of unusual quality ... has an unusual devil. You must get to know your personal devil. You must even get to know his father, the Old Devil.
(*Fifth Business*)

"Is it my imagination or are you frowning, Zadkiel?" Maimas asked, poking the angel.

"What, with your talk about elitism," Zadkiel observed, "it has occurred to me that Robertson is removed from the world, and I'm not sure if I respect such withdrawal."

"I can't guess what you're referring to, old boy," Maimas responded with irritating confidence.

"He has buried himself in a graduate college where he wipes the noses of sheltered types like himself. He pays no attention to the events about him. I mean, he wilfully blinded himself to the Cuban Missile Crisis of 1961 — that staring match between the U.S. and Russia that almost triggered a nuclear war — as well as those developments in Vietnam, the assassination of the U.S. president, and the terrible conflict in the Middle East."

"Don't be so cantankerous and stuffy, Zadkiel. Artists are contradictory types. On the one hand, they are full of themselves and blind to the boiling lava about them; yet they manage to set our humanity in relief and capture its meaning with such overarching beauty that who can blame them if they fail to comment on the chaff of our lives?"

"With all due respect, Maimas, Davies' Salterton Trilogy and dramas are interesting, to be sure, but in my humble opinion they are not in the top tier of artistic endeavour."

"I quite agree. That why his life's next chapter is so instrumental."

It was a blustery day in October 1970. Davies was seated at the desk in his office and was glancing out the window at the Massey College courtyard. A caretaker was removing the goldfish from the pond to store them in a warmer place for the length of the winter. One of the senior fellows, an ancient historian, was going through his regular exercise routine while a short distance off three students were throwing a Frisbee, all of them dressed in shorts and T-shirts despite the hint of frost in the air.

At the same time, a radio was playing somewhere in the background and was tuned to the news. Its lead story was shocking. Members of the terrorist group *Front de Libération du Québec* (FLQ) had murdered Quebec minister of labour, Pierre Laporte, whom they had kidnapped one week earlier from his home in Montreal. This same group was holding British trade commissioner James Cross hostage in an effort to further their separatist dreams. They would not release him until the police freed their "brothers," who had been arrested over several months on a number of charges. The death of Pierre Laporte, the broadcast continued, was triggered by Prime Minister Trudeau's invoking of the War Measures Act the day before — an act that granted the police wide powers of arrest and detainment. And troops would be deployed to various cities in Quebec to guard federal buildings and their employees.

Davies sighed. To distract himself from these chilling events, he gazed at the book that was lying on his desk. It had arrived from the publisher just minutes before, the editor having received it from the printer that same morning. Its cover featured a stylish magician beneath the book's stark title: *Fifth Business*. Davies nodded to himself, leaned back in his chair, and reflected on the image that had initially led him to create the novel.

This image or vision dated back to 1958 — just when Jungian psychology had begun to obsess him. It had consisted of a snowy street in Thamesville, Ontario, where he had passed his early childhood. Two boys had been quarrelling. After insulting his pal, one of them had run away, while the offended party had rolled himself a snowball. Catching up with his friend, he had flung the snowball at him and would have hit him, too, had the boy not ducked and allowed the ball to strike a pregnant woman instead. And so a strange chain of events was put into effect.

"Good drama, that," Davies was thinking to himself.

He was thinking, too, how he'd surprised himself, as well as Brenda when she read his early drafts, when he started writing the story in 1968. The tale was so different from his other writing. Simply put, it was as if he had opened up his head and emptied its contents onto sheets of blank paper. His own story was present, much modified of course, together with his interest in saints, Jungian psychology, his European travels, his belief in coincidence and, most important, his love of magic. He had not been sure he could hold this material together, but like Magnus Eisengrim, his fictional magician, he had carried off this act of ... prestidigitation.

The story is told as a letter, which seventy-year-old Dunstan Ramsay writes to his "boss," the headmaster of Colborne College, where Ramsay has taught history for forty-five years. In this letter Ramsay wishes to prove that, far from having lived a sequestered life, he has experienced his fair share of adventure and discovery.

Ramsay's life story starts in the town of Deptford with the snowball episode when he is ten years old. Percy "Boy" Staunton throws a snowball at him, he ducks, and Mary Dempster, who is pregnant, is struck full in the head. The accident leads her to deliver her son prematurely — his name is Paul — and in subsequent years her behaviour is affected. Besides neglecting her household, she wanders Deptford in a state of undress and dispenses charity she can ill afford. More scandalously, she is discovered one night having sex with a hobo in the town's gravel pit. When asked by her husband why she has behaved so strangely, she answers that the man wanted it so badly and she simply had not the heart to refuse.

Ramsay feels responsible for this chain of events. As the Dempster household steadily worsens, he entertains Paul and introduces him to magic: whereas his own hands are thick and clumsy, Paul proves a natural magician. He also falls in love with Mrs. Dempster and convinces himself she is a modern-day saint, not only because of her charitable disposition, but because (as he sees it) she has been able to restore his dead brother to life.

The First World War erupts and Ramsay joins the army. In one incident he performs heroically but loses a leg, and only survives the ordeal (he believes) because he prays to a statue of the Virgin Mary, whose face is the spitting image of Mary Dempster's. When the war is over, Ramsay becomes a teacher back in Canada. He resumes his friendship with Percy "Boy" Staunton, loses his childhood sweetheart to him, and watches as his friend becomes a leading Canadian businessman and industrialist. Over the years, Boy's external success is matched by Ramsay's internal progress: the latter becomes a renowned expert on saints, to the point that he writes several books on them, even as he discovers in the process truths about himself and the world at large. His introspection and hard-won wisdom eventually clash with Boy's materialistic outlook:

> "Don't nag me, Dunny," [Boy] said. "I feel rotten. I've done just about everything I've ever planned to do, and everybody thinks I'm a success. And of course I have Denyse [his second wife] now to keep me up to the mark, which is lucky — damned lucky, and don't imagine I don't feel it. But sometimes I wish I could get into a car and drive away from the whole damned thing."
>
> "... You'll have to grow old, Boy; you'll have to find out what age means, and how to be old. A

dear old friend of mine once told me he wanted a God who would teach him how to grow old. I expect he found what he wanted. You must do the same, or be wretched. Whom the gods hate they keep forever young."

He looked at me almost with hatred. "That's the most lunatic defeatist nonsense I've ever heard in my life," he said.

It is in his travels that Ramsay meets up with Paul Dempster, on the first occasion when he is part of a travelling show, then later when he has flowered into the world-renowned Magnus Eisengrim. Through Magnus, the aging Ramsay will encounter the magician's manager, Liesl Vitziputzli, an aristocratic woman of hideous aspect, who hires Ramsay to write a mock biography of Magnus and, after a rough wrestling match, wins Ramsay as her lover. The troupe then travels to Toronto where, in the book's climactic scene, Ramsay discloses to Boy Staunton and Paul that the snowball from so many years back had hidden at its middle an egg-sized stone, one that he has in his possession still. The next morning Boy Staunton's car is dragged from Lake Ontario, with his corpse at the wheel, the incriminating stone in his mouth.

As had been the case with his Salterton Trilogy, Davies filled his novel with autobiographical elements. The town of Deptford was based on his hometown Thamesville, to the degree that the layout of each was a perfect match. Ramsay's attempts to instruct Paul in magic were drawn from Davies's own experiments as a boy: like Ramsay, Davies possessed a clumsy set of hands. The Madonna that Ramsay spies at the battle of Passchendaele is identical to the statue that Davies purchased on a trip to Austria.

And then there is the following passage, which was entirely lifted from Davies's clashes with his mother:

> She pursued me around the kitchen, slashing me with the whip until she broke down and I cried. She cried, too, hysterically, and beat me harder, storming about my impudence, my want of respect for her, of my increasing oddity and intellectual arrogance ... until at last her fury was spent, and she ran upstairs in tears and banged the door of her bedroom....
>
> My father and Willie [Ramsay's brother] came home, and there was no supper. Naturally he sided with her, and Willie was very officious and knowing about how intolerable I had become of late, and how thrashing was too good for me. Finally it was decided that my mother would come downstairs if I would beg pardon. This I had to do on my knees, repeating a formula improvised by my father, which included a pledge that I would always love my mother, to whom I owed the great gift of life.

The most powerful autobiographical component, however, was Ramsay's certainty that the realm of mystery, spirit, and awe co-exists with the more ordinary realm of science, law, work, and pragmatism. Just as Davies believed that Jung's collective unconscious and archetypes explained human initiative and destiny, linking everyday experiences to religion, art, mythology, and literature, so Ramsay discovers that magic and a more mythic and less factual approach to history, together with saints and their inspiring tales of faith and miracles, provide a powerful foundation for human endeavour and identity. Neither man has achieved the same status as Boy Staunton or Rupert Davies, but his internal journey has taught each of them fundamental truths about the human condition, and this knowledge proves more enduring and uplifting than mere wealth and power. In other words, neither villain nor hero in the opera of life, Ramsay, like Davies, is fifth business.

"I like the structure of *Fifth Business*," an admirer informed Davies at the launch for his novel. This was on a boat in the Toronto Harbour close to the spot where Boy Staunton had driven his car into the lake. "I like the way you wrote the book as a letter."

"Thank you. I appreciate your kind remarks."

"I was just wondering why Dunstan Ramsay addresses himself to his boss, the headmaster of Colborne College —"

"Oh no no no. He does no such thing."

"Really? Don't you tell us at the start of your novel that —"

"Yes, I mention his headmaster as the letter's recipient, but that's a pure literary dodge."

"I don't understand."

"I see you don't. The letter's actual recipient is God himself, my good man."

The public response to *Fifth Business* far exceeded Davies's expectations. In 1970, at the age of fifty-seven, Davies had a reputation within Canada as a man of letters to be sure, and had won some visibility for himself in the United States and England, but he was regarded as a literary talent of the preceding generation — an old-fashioned, middling talent at that. *Fifth Business* changed everything. Many influential publications in North America were full of praise for his novel: the *New Yorker* described *Fifth Business* as "elegant"; the *New York Times* wrote of it as "a marvellously energetic novel ... driven by inevitable narrative force"; *Esquire* described it as "as masterfully executed as anything in the history of the novel." Internationally renowned authors Saul Bellow, John Fowles, and Anthony Burgess praised *Fifth Business* to the skies, with predictable results. Davies became a celebrity and his novel a bestseller. Having been cloistered in his Massey College office for twelve years, Davies was suddenly deluged with requests to give speeches, readings, and interviews.

"With me this morning is Canada's own Robertson Davies, author of the best-selling *Fifth Business*," a well-known CBC radio host announced shortly after the novel's publication.

"It's a pleasure to be here."

"Now, I realize you're a busy man and have other interviews to rush off to, so I'll keep this brief. *Fifth Business* is doing well?"

"It is faring beyond my wildest expectations."

"You must be delighted. But tell me, what is it about *Fifth Business* that has struck such a nerve, more so than any of your previous novels?"

"I write extensively about saints and our religious instincts in *Fifth Business*; readers seem to like this subject. And then there is the story of the magician Paul Dempster. If you wish to win an audience over, throw in some magic. On a more serious note, however, there is my characters' preoccupation with death."

"Death? That surprises me. Our age doesn't like to talk about such things."

"Yes, quite right. And that's precisely why I wished to set it at the heart of my story. There are many deaths in *Fifth Business*, both literal and figurative. Dunstan Ramsay is obsessed with the subject; he sees it as a cornerstone of human existence, and I think my readers share this point of view."

"To judge by the sales figure, you must be right."

"Magic and death: it's a heady combination."

Davies's mind-boggling success led his publisher to ask for a repeat performance, and quickly at that. Still burdened with the task of running Massey College and teaching his literature courses, Davies set to work on another novel, which he had started taking notes for already. Although he was not planning a sequel to *Fifth Business*, he was intent on reusing some of its main characters, and exploring certain Jungian ideas in greater depth, as well as examining the relationship between a father and his full-grown son. Over time his approach became clear to him; the book found him, as he liked to describe the writing process.

In the last scene of *Fifth Business*, as Magnus is performing his trick "The Brazen Head of Friar Bacon," in which audience members ask a "levitated" head of brass any question that comes to mind, someone yells, "Who killed Boy Staunton?" Davies reveals in his second novel that the speaker was David Staunton, Boy Staunton's forty-year-old son. An accomplished lawyer and alcoholic, David is at odds with himself. Shocked by his father's death, but at the same crippled by his early upraising — Boy was intent on making a "man" of his son, but one in his own spiritually bankrupt image — David travels to Zurich where, in contrast to his habitual aloofness, he chooses to subject himself to an intense round of Jungian analysis.

His analyst is Dr. Johanna Von Haller. Her procedure is to elicit from him long narratives of his history, then subject these episodes to examination through a Socratic-like technique of question and answer. Resenting the fact he is being treated by a woman, and intensely skeptical of the process itself, David is defensive in his initial sessions. He subjects the doctor's statements to his own interrogations, as if he were questioning a witness in court, and rejects the conclusion she steers him toward — that his father was a superficial man with no concept or interest in his own inner workings, and by consequence a dreadful parent. Gradually she demonstrates that Boy's refusal to grant his son an adequate allowance, his countless affairs, his initiation of David into the mysteries of sex through the services of a courtesan, and his insistence that life's priorities consist of wealth, power, and physical pleasure amounted to intrusions on David's fragile psyche and explained his alcoholism and instability. As she says of people like David's father:

> We all create an outward self with which to face the world, and some people come to believe that is what they truly are. So they people the world with doctors who are nothing outside the consulting-room, and judges who are nothing when they are not in court, and businessmen who wither with boredom when they have to retire from business, and teachers who are forever teaching. That is why they are such poor specimens when they are caught without their masks on. They have lived chiefly though the Persona. But you are not such a fool, or you would not be here.

And having released him from the need to believe in his father's greatness, Dr. Haller triggers his awareness of the way certain Jungian archetypes have appeared to him throughout his life — the Magus, the Shadow, the Anima, and others.

And then the story shifts. While touring the Swiss town of St. Gall, David runs into Dunstan Ramsay, who was his father's friend and his own history teacher at Colborne College. Although David thinks this has happened by chance, Ramsay tells him, "As an historian I don't believe in coincidence. Only very rigid minds do.... I suppose you had to meet us for some reason. A good one, I hope." Ramsay is living with Paul Dempster and Liesl Vitziputzli, as the troupe's residential philosopher, and the trio invites David to stay with them at Liesl's castle, Sorgenfrei.

In the course of his visit, David learns from Magnus that his father, far from having been killed by the magician, expressed the keen desire to step on his car's accelerator and abandon his life's complications. As a favour, Magnus granted him this wish. Ramsay in turn reveals to him that a man can have many fathers, and not merely the biological progenitor. Teachers, mentors, and protectors — all of these can play the role of father. As a way of ending the trauma of Boy Staunton's death, moreover, Ramsay throws over a mountainside the stone that was planted by Boy in the snowball, and that he has carried with him everywhere these many years. And finally there is Liesl's influence ...

Davies was planning a big, climactic sense of discovery but, as he sat down to write the scene, its details escaped him.

"Are you just about finished?" Brenda asked him a few days after Christmas 1971.

"It's that ending. It keeps eluding me."

"You'll have to come up with something. Your deadline's approaching and your publisher is getting antsy. He phoned just an hour ago."

"I know. I know. But the ending just won't come."

He kept grappling with ideas, but none of them fit. Then one night he happened to be reading, even as he nibbled on a bear-shaped cookie from St. Gall (these had been on hand through all of Christmas). The book was one by the mythologist

Joseph Campbell, and the chapter Davies was looking over was about a prehistoric bear cult that had been discovered in caves across northern Europe. Davies looked up from his book and glanced down at his cookie. A moment later he was at his desk and typing furiously. He had his climatic ending.

Liesl conducts David to a cave in the Alps, and then down into a remote recess, at great risk to the pair of them. There, she explains, their ancient ancestors once worshipped the bear. When David expresses little interest in her words, she douses the light and forces him to exert himself if he is to escape that mountain cave alive. He barely manages the near-impossible climb and, in his fear, soils himself. The effect of the adventure is cathartic, however:

> I was bathed and in bed by five o'clock, dead
> beat. But so miraculous is the human spirit, I
> was up and about and able to eat a good dinner
> and watch a Christmas broadcast from Lausanne
> with Ramsay and Eisengrim and Liesl, renewed
> — yes, and it seemed to be reborn, by the terror
> of the cave and the great promise she had made
> to me a few hours before.

With the climax in place, and the manuscript submitted, all that remained was the novel's title.

"I rather like your proposed title, *Son and Stranger*, but at the same think we can do better than that," his editor informed him.

"What did you have in mind?" Davies growled, always leery of an editor's attempts to improve on his efforts.

"I'm not quite sure. Something catchier but at the same time mystical. Maybe a symbol of sorts, something buried in medieval lore, but representative of the complexities of Jungian theory. Do you follow me?"

"No."

"Here's an example of what I mean: the manticore."

"The manticore?"

"It's a creature of legend, a bit like the sphinx, with the head of a human and a lion's body —"

"I know what a bloody manticore is!"

"It's just a suggestion. There's no sense losing your temper —"

"I like it. It's perfect. Say goodbye to *Son and Stranger* and hello to *The Manticore.*"

Fifth Business was a hard act to follow, but the critical response to *The Manticore* proved Davies had carried it off. The novel was greeted with a slew of positive reviews. While the *Globe and Mail* found the book tedious, the *Toronto Star*, the *Chicago Tribune*, the *New York Times*, *Newsweek*, and a large number of other papers extolled the novel. Like *Fifth Business*, it sold exceptionally well, for a literary work, and earned Davies a Governor General's Award — long overdue, by some admirers' estimates. Most important, it encouraged Davies to round his two Deptford novels off with a final sequel.

Even as he set about writing this third book, he was embroiled in a bitter dispute at Massey College. The majority of students refused to accept the fact that the college was a refuge for male academics and voted to allow it to go co-ed. Again and again they tried to force the issue, and Davies, convinced this innovation would be a betrayal of Vincent Massey's wishes, refused to relent. When students proposed that Massey's relatives be consulted — Vincent Massey had died in 1967 — again Davies refused to give in.

"You're bothered by this quarrel, aren't you?" his daughter Miranda asked him in the course of a phone call.

"Is that why you phoned? You're lining up for your pound of flesh, along with all the other demolition experts?"

"No. I'm phoning because I've finished reading *Fifth Business* and *The Manticore.*"

"Oh."

"And I wanted to tell you, not only that the books transported me, but that you took me by surprise."

"How so?"

"When I was growing up, you were always telling me to mind my manners, and wear my skirts low and my blouses high."

"And damned good advice it was."

"And here you are writing about a woman who has sex with a tramp, and a deformed giant who likes girls, but has a go at Ramsay, and other hilarious and experimental situations. Do you know what you are in your books? You're a swinger."

"I don't know how to answer that."

"And, incidentally, you'll lose this battle over the co-ed status of Massey College. But you'll come to realize your defeat was no big deal."

Miranda proved prescient. Davies was forced to admit female students into Massey College in 1973 and, once they had settled in, he understood that it was not the end of the world. And when this squabble was over, he had a free hand to focus on his third Deptford novel.

"So what's it about?" Brenda asked, depositing a cup of tea on his desk.

"I want to bring a variety of ingredients to bear. First, I have unfinished business with Paul and should finally tell the story of his unhappy childhood."

"Why does his childhood have to be unhappy?"

"Because hardship allows us to see to the heart of certain matters. Besides, he will turn his hard origins to good account."

"Through magic?"

"Yes."

"And when's the story taking place?"

"It starts in our present, but Paul is recounting his early days, near the turn of the century. Such a timeline will allow me to discuss our country's early, formative years. Because our population has changed over the last two decades, with people arriving from all over the globe, it's easy for Canadians to forget the English effect on our identity, and in my view that's a terribly pity."

"So the book is about a magician's apprenticeship and the Canada of bygone days?"

"Yes, but there's more to it than that."

"Of course there is. You're Robertson Davies."

Like its predecessors, the finished narrative was full of twists and turns. The novel opens on a BBC crew that has engaged Paul Dempster to play the role of the nineteenth-century magician Robert Houdin in a film documentary. Between shoots in Switzerland, and later London, Paul/Eisengrim has exchanges with this crew, together with Ramsay, who is on hand to observe the proceedings. In the course of their conversations he reveals the details of his past.

His first step into his life as a performer occurred when he strayed into a circus tent in Deptford, was sexually abused by the magician Willard, then kidnapped by this same man and forced to wander the country as a member of this sideshow. This carnival consisted of the usual fare: a bearded lady, a monkey act, a strong man, a contortionist, and the like. Paul's own contribution was to sit inside a large mechanical device nicknamed Abdullah and beat the audience at cards. After years of this apprenticeship, he emerged as a master mechanic and a first-rate conjuror.

This circus fell apart over time, and Paul escaped to Europe with Willard (who was an incurable morphine addict) and toured the continent with yet another circus. It was in the course of his travels that he met up with Ramsay. When this venture proved unsustainable, he won a junior position with the London theatre company of Sir John Tresize and his wife Milady (who were based on the real-life actors Sir John Martin-Harvey and Miss N. de Silva). Here Paul received instruction in the techniques of the Victorian stage and participated in a variety of melodramatic productions, accompanying the theatre troupe on a cross-Canada tour, and acquiring a worldly, less antagonistic demeanour.

After Sir John's death, he found work as an expert clock mechanic, and was subsequently hired by a Swiss aristocrat to repair his collection of rare, mechanical toys — ones that his daughter had broken in a fit of rage. This young woman was Liesl, who suffered from acromegaly and was monstrously tall and had an ape-like facial appearance. While effecting repairs, Paul was attacked by this "creature" but, trained in dirty fighting from his years at the circus, subdued Liesl and befriended her. He also caused her to refine her behaviour and, eventually, the pair created their *Soirée des Illusions*, an epic show that established Paul's reputation as the world's leading magician.

In the book's last scene, once Paul/Eisengrim's narrative has ended and the documentary has been completed, Ramsay, Liesl, and Paul lie together in bed and enjoy a final philosophical exchange. Paul is given the last word and he sums his position up as follows:

> [Life is] pretty much like a World of Wonders....
> Everything has its astonishing, wondrous as-
> pect, if you bring a mind to it that's really
> your own — a mind that hasn't been smeared
> and blurred with half-understood muck from
> schools, or the daily papers, or any other ragbag
> of reach-me-down notions.

World of Wonders appeared in October 1975. Again, the critic-al response was overwhelmingly positive. Some critics believed that Davies had accomplished the impossible and surpassed the first two volumes of the Deptford Trilogy. He was even referred to not only as the finest living Canadian novelist, but as one of the most accomplished novelists of his generation. Book sales were prodigious, not only in the English-speaking world, but across Europe as a whole, as the trilogy was translated into a variety of languages. Despite the complication of his plots, his puzzling ref-erences to an arcane body of knowledge, and his appeal to art and mysticism and disavowal of reason — or perhaps because of these same elements — the demand for his work was insatiable.

"Excuse me. May I please speak to Mr. Robertson Davies?" a stranger asked, calling Davies at his Windhover home.

"This is he. With whom am I speaking?"

"My name is Paula and I'm a Grade Thirteen student from Barrie, Ontario."

"I'm pleased to meet you, Paula. How can I help you?"

"Well, my English teacher, Mrs. Brighton, finished reading your latest novel *World of Wonders* two months ago. She liked it so much that she decided to assign it to our class, and tomorrow I have an essay due but I don't know what to write about it. That's why I've phoned."

"I see."

"So can you tell me what your novel is about?"

"I can try, I suppose. The theme of self-discovery is important, of course. But what I really wanted to get at was the transformational quality of art."

"Mrs. Brighton will like that. It sounds impressive. But what do you mean?"

"Well, think about it. As he passes through all his experiences, Paul comes to understand that, side by side with the world of ordinary, daily events, lurks an invisible reality that is both terrifying and beautiful. Humans can sometimes grasp this reality through religion and worship, but art is an effective avenue as well. More than anyone, in fact, or so Paul concludes, artists like Magnus Eisengrim, through their remarkable skills and acts of deception, lead their audiences to glimpse this invisible world and gape in wonder. And once this invisible world is descried, the viewer's sense of self becomes infinitely stronger."

"That's all?"

"I'm afraid so. It's not enough?"

"It will only do me for one paragraph, and the essay has to be two pages long."

It was not only high school students who clamoured to have his novels explained to them. Invitations arrived from a range of institutions for Davies to give readings from his novels or to share his views on an array of topics; indeed, such was the appetite for his various insights that he published a selection of his talks in 1977 in a book entitled *One Half of Robertson Davies*. While delighted with this response to his efforts, and happy to lap up the attention and critical praise, Davies did not allow these new demands on his time to interfere unduly with his primary work.

His imagination as explosive as ever, he was already at work on a fresh trilogy.

8

The Cornish Trilogy

Paleo-psychology: It's really digging into what people thought, in times when their thinking was a muddle of religion and folk-belief and rags of misunderstood classical learning; instead of being what it is today, which I suppose you'd have to call a muddle of materialism, and folk-belief, and rags of misunderstood scientific learning.
(*The Rebel Angels*)

Civilization rests on two things: the discovery that fermentation produces alcohol, and the voluntary ability to inhibit defecation.
(*The Rebel Angels*)

Davies and Vincent Massey in the Common Room at Massey College. September 1963. Photo by Jack Marshall Ltd.

Scholars are mendicants. Always have been, and
always will be — or so I hope. God help us all if
they ever got control of any real money.
(*The Rebel Angels*)

Biography at its best is a form of fiction.
(*The Lyre of Orpheus*)

"So your boy has finally made it, Maimas old chap. Congratulations.
I had my doubts that your meddling would push him along, but I'm
delighted to see you have proven me wrong."

"Thank you, Zadkiel. That's the hardest part about being an angel.
You strain on behalf of your protégé, then he meets with success and
people adore him, yet people forget you were his inspiration."

"Still, I suppose he can take it easy now. He can coast and watch
as the laurels come in."

"My dear Zadkiel, forgive me for saying so, but you clearly don't know
how the writer's mind works. Having raised the bar of his writing so high,
Robertson was determined to prop it even higher. And far from sitting
back and enjoying his fame, he worried himself sick achieving this goal."

"They're dreadful creatures, these busy humans."

"You're right, old man, and the writers are the worst of the lot."

It was hot summer day in 1981. Again Davies was seated in his
office at Massey College and staring out the window to the
courtyard beyond. Some students were throwing a ball around,
while a friend of theirs strummed on his guitar, playing several
bars of Bach then changing over to Bob Dylan. The pools, the
courtyard lawn, and, dimly visible, the school's bell tower were
strikingly beautiful, or seemed so at that moment.

A radio was blaring in the courtyard and describing an Israeli attack on the PLO in Lebanon, then recounting how a walkway in a Kansas hotel had collapsed and killed 114 people. Davies sighed. More bad news. He was feeling old and very unsettled because his tenure as master was reaching an end: he was almost seventy and it was time to retire.

In some ways he was happy to leave the college behind. Retirement would give him more time to write and, in truth, he sometimes found university life a little too cloistered. While the ivory tower was home to a group of extraordinary scholars, it was often used by shy, retiring types as a refuge from the world outside. And his views, always a little old-fashioned, were at variance with the sentiment among the staff and student body. A firm believer in personal responsibility, Davies was at odds with the many fellows who had "progressive" ideas about crime, the arts, marriage, and family. On the other hand, his years at Massey College had been happy and productive ones. He would miss rubbing shoulders with the student population, and engaging senior fellows in debates on a wide array of fascinating subjects, from physics to the cost of cheese in medieval Venice. Most of all, he regretted growing old. His hair by now was a shocking white and his movements were slow, painstaking, and cumbersome — exactly what one would expect of a man nearing seventy.

The one consolation as he dwelled upon retirement was the book lying on the desk before him. It was a copy, hot off the press, of his latest novel, *The Rebel Angels*. As always, it gave him a thrill to see in final form the narrative that, some twelve months back, had been mere ideas drifting about in limbo. He smiled, remembering his and Brenda's excursion to the Rosedale neighbourhood to find a retirement property they could live in and at the same time rent to tenants.

"I told you we shouldn't enter this place," Brenda had commented as they had toured a relic from the Edwardian age. "It hasn't been repaired in years, or cleaned, for that matter."

"What peculiar tenants," Davies replied. "How many cats do you think that old lady owns?"

"More than she can properly care for. Even if you scrubbed for days on end, you would never get rid of this awful smell."

"And that brother and sister we saw in the basement. What do you suppose their story is?"

"They were from Eastern Europe and they looked like gypsies. Did you see the socks soaking in the kitchen sink? And there were wood shavings scattered on the living-room floor."

"I didn't notice. I was taken with the violins on the kitchen table. There were five of them, two with their guts exposed. And did you notice the tarot cards over to one side?"

"Let's leave. This is an awful place. I would never buy a property like this."

"I wouldn't either. But it has certainly stirred my imagination."

He had started gathering notes for his book as early as 1976, but had not begun the actual writing until the spring of 1979. By the time he was ready to set the story down, he knew he wished to draw a detailed portrait of the university, celebrating its medieval origins, its spirit of inquiry, and its centrality to Western civilization, even as he described its less admirable aspects — the feuding between professors, the pedantry of academic life, and its encouragement of credentialism and hostility to anything non-rational in nature.

In keeping with this theme — that universities were too quick to dismiss non-rational pursuits — he was intent on fitting the medieval thinker Paracelsus into his story, as well as alchemy, tarot cards, gypsies and their wisdom, astrology, the writer Rabelais, and, never squeamish in his literary efforts, the transformative effects of human feces.

And so, *The Rebel Angels* took shape. Its setting is Coulter College, a reproduction of Massey College, just as the adjoining St. John and the Holy Ghost is a stand-in for Trinity College (at the University of Toronto). Maria Magdalena Theotoky is a graduate student of gypsy descent who is studying under Professor Clement Hollier, a paleo-psychologist whose research is designed to reveal how medieval people perceived their world. The pair is joined by a friend of Hollier's, John Parlabane, a brilliant philosopher who has just "escaped" from a monastery and, with nowhere else to go, sets up camp in Hollier's office where he assails Maria with his egotism and skeptical view of the world.

Parlabane's insidious effects on Maria's equanimity are offset by the warmth and scholarship of Simon Darcourt, an Anglican priest who has set himself the task of writing brief biographies of the university's faculty members. At the same time Simon, together with Hollier and the Renaissance scholar Urquhart McVarish, have been appointed executors of collector Francis Cornish's estate, which consists of paintings, artifacts, and old manuscripts, including one by the French author Rabelais. Maria is desperate to procure this manuscript and use it as the basis for a doctoral thesis, but it mysteriously vanishes — Darcourt and Hollier suspect McVarish has grabbed it.

At one point Hollier inveigles Maria to introduce him to her mother, a bona fide gypsy who is a tarot card reader, fiddler, and violin expert — she repairs these instruments by steeping them in horse excrement. Excrement, of the human strain, surfaces again as a topic of interest in the experiments of Professor Ozzy Froats, who believes (almost in an alchemical strain) that this loathsome substance can be put to therapeutic use.

The story's climax is twofold. Provoked beyond endurance by the repulsive Urquhart McVarish, with whom he has endured a masochistic affair, Parlabane brutally murders the professor. These events are described in a letter that Parlabane leaves at the scene of his own death: the doctor suspects suicide, but there is no proof of this. On a more positive note, Maria marries Arthur Cornish, the nephew and heir of Francis Cornish. Her scholarly dealings with Hollier, and the academic's cerebral approach to the world, have taught her that she cannot focus on mere intellect, but must allow other human capacities to flourish.

And the book's title? Where did that come from? Davies explains its meaning in an exchange between Maria and Simon Darcourt, who has himself proposed to Maria and been rebuffed. In a conciliatory talk, Maria comforts Darcourt even as she explains how universities came about:

> Oh Simon, you must remember the Rebel Angels? They were real angels, Samahazai and Azazel, and they betrayed the secrets of Heaven to King Solomon, and God threw them out of Heaven. And did they mope and plot vengeance? Not they! They weren't sore-headed egotists like Lucifer. Instead they gave mankind another push up the ladder, they came to earth and taught tongues, and healing and laws and hygiene — taught everything — and they were often special successes with "the daughters of men." It's a marvellous piece of apocrypha, and I would have expected you to know it, because surely it is the explanation of the origin of universities! God doesn't come out in these stories

in a very good light, does He? Job had to tell him a few home truths about His injustice and caprice; the Rebel Angels showed him that hiding all knowledge and wisdom and keeping it for Himself was dog-in-the-manger behaviour. I've always taken it as proof that we'll civilize God yet.

"*The Rebel Angels* is a great novel," Davies overheard one student say to another. He was sitting in the Trinity cafeteria, and was hidden behind the *New York Times*.

"It's a godawful mess," his friend retorted. "You have all these characters making grand pronouncements, and a hodgepodge of supposedly learned topics, but there isn't any central theme."

"Of course there's a central theme. Understanding and enlightenment can be discovered in materials that, at first glance, seem ridiculous, disgusting even. It's like the alchemist's touchstone that can turn lead into gold."

"Are you talking about Ozzy Froats' experiments with crap?"

"That's part of it, as is Mamusia's use of horse dung to fix violins, and the truths that astrology and tarot cards can reveal. Maria sees her gypsy mother as an embarrassing relic from a primitive culture, someone who has no place in her world of the mind, yet she learns to see how the commonplace is in actual fact extraordinary."

"Jesus! Listen to you! You're even talking like one of his uptight characters!"

"Thank you very much. I'll take that as a compliment."

Despite its academic and empathetic tone, *The Rebel Angels* revealed a vindictive spark on Davies's part: he was someone who believed in taking vengeance on one's enemies. From an early age he had associated God with vengeful qualities: detesting the "feminine," forgiving Jesus, he had concentrated more on the Old Testament's angry overlord who punishes transgressions in an unforgiving manner. In later life, in a chat with his students, Davies had playfully stated that he approved of capital punishment on the grounds that it allowed society to seek revenge from its outcasts. In *Tempest-Tost*, moreover, Davies had parodied his former mathematics teacher at Upper Canada College, Mr. Mc-Kenzie, in the character of Hector Mackilwraith who buffoonishly tries to hang himself. And the theme of "getting even" had been present in *Fifth Business* — Paul Dempster and Ramsay conspire, very subtly, to bring an end to Boy Staunton. In *The Rebel Angels*, however, this hankering for vengeance was more pointed and personal than on previous occasions.

His character Urquhart McVarish was closely modelled on his former colleague (and nemesis) Professor W.A.C.H. Dobson. Dobson was a brilliant scholar of Chinese culture and, convinced he had been robbed of the mastership of Massey College, had made life difficult for Davies by supporting students who had found the atmosphere at Massey overly confining. The relationship between the two men reached a boiling point on a winter night in 1969 — nicknamed the "Night of the Green Ghost" by Massey students — when Davies, wearing nothing more than a green dressing gown, broke in on a late-night revel hosted by Dobson. Although he could not dismiss Dobson on the spot, Davies did orchestrate his removal three years later, when the "rabble-rouser's" senior fellowship came up for renewal. Still smarting from the effects of Dobson's meddling years later, Davies decided to manhandle him in his novel.

"I've just finished reading your *Rebel Angels*," an old friend and university colleague told Davies. "I like it immensely, but —"

"But ...?"

"It's that character of yours, Urquhart McVarish. He's based on Dobson, isn't he? I mean, he claims to be of high-born descent, he boasts about his war record, he wears a hairnet at night, and is, overall, quite dreadful to deal with."

"I'm admitting nothing. But what of it?"

"Well, the way you kill him off is blood-chilling. You embarrass the guy by involving him in a strange sexual encounter, then stuff a knitting needle up his nose. It's shocking, Rob."

"That's the point. I intended to shock. Shocking readers gladdens my soul."

The critical response to *The Rebel Angels* was for the most part positive. Some critics felt that Davies was overly pedantic, that his dialogue was designed more to illustrate Davies's personal interests than to capture the inner workings of his characters, and that there was too much talk of excrement. Other reviewers strongly disagreed. John Kenneth Galbraith, the renowned Canadian economist, extolled *The Rebel Angels* in a long article in a New York publication, while Anthony Burgess, the British writer best known for his novel *A Clockwork Orange*, expressed the belief that Davies should receive the Nobel Prize.

The day of Davies's retirement dawned. To celebrate his enormous contributions to the college, the staff organized several farewell parties. One friend and fellow academic had written a play for Davies, based on snippets from his own theatrical productions, and had it performed by members the Hart House Drama Centre. While most members of the audience were bewildered, Davies was delighted and could not contain his laughter. There was also a musical rendition by the Massey College

Singers of Davies's favourite Victorian songs. And then there were the gifts: the complete monthly segments of Charles Dickens' *Little Dorrit*, a handcrafted wooden lectern, a pair of silver urns, and the renaming of the college's library to The Robertson Davies Library. A fund-drive for this same library was started, and huge sums of money were gathered when donors learned they were contributing money in Davies's name. He received an Honorary Doctor of Laws from the University of Toronto — the fifteenth honorary doctorate to be bestowed on him.

And through it all, he continued writing. In addition to his usual public talks and readings, he delivered the prestigious Alexander Lectures at the University of Toronto and had this material on nineteenth-century theatre published in book form. He also put together a collection of his annual ghost stories at the Massey College Christmas Gaudy — it was entitled *High Spirits*. And he tried his hand at writing the libretto for a children's opera (*Dr. Canon's Cure*), the music for which was written by Canadian composer Derek Holman. Most important, he pressed on with his *genuine* writing: he was already at work on yet another novel.

"I can't provide you with any details yet," Davies told his agent, Elizabeth Sifton, on the eve of his departure for a two-week art tour of Europe, led by experts from the Art Gallery of Ontario. "But it will be a prequel to *The Rebel Angels*, and not a sequel. And it will be about the life of a painter."

"Is that why you're off to Europe on that art tour?"

"Yes. I don't know art the way I know literature and music."

"Then why make your central character a painter?"

"Because it's something new, and my detractors complain that I'm always reconstituting the same old subjects. This time I'll show them."

"One last question, Rob. Do you ever suffer from writer's block?"

"I'm afraid my affliction is the opposite. I have too many narratives swimming about in my head."

"Have a great trip. And watch out for those German wines; they're addictive and pack a terrific punch."

The story that unfolded was more pointed than *The Rebel Angels*, yet still full of Davies's idiosyncratic verve and learning. The novel opens with a discussion between Simon Darcourt and the recently married Cornishes, Arthur and Maria, who have hired Darcourt to write a biography of Francis Cornish. To his dismay, Simon cannot find any solid material about his subject, but cannot shake the feeling that there is a ripping good tale to be told. Even as he leaves the Cornish residence in a state of frustration, Francis Cornish's *true* biography is revealed by the Daimon Maimas and the Lesser Zadkiel.

Cornish is the son of Mary-Jim McRory, from the Ontario lumber-town Blairlogie, and the Englishman Major Francis Cornish who, on discovering Mary-Jim had become pregnant after a brief dalliance with a stranger, offered to marry her if her wealthy father provided him with a substantial income. The product of the illicit affair, Francis Junior discovers later in life, is a half-wit child (also named Francis!) who ostensibly died the year after his birth but in actual fact has survived and been kept upstairs in the family attic, far removed from the public eye.

Francis's own childhood is anxiety-ridden. A lonely child — his parents are always travelling abroad — he discovers at an early stage that he has an artist's eye. Teaching himself to draw from an old, artist's how-to manual, he perfects his technique by regularly sketching the corpses in a funeral parlour run by the affable Zadok Hoyle. Eventually he is dispatched by his parents to Colborne College in Toronto (again a stand-in for Upper Canada College), where he wins a prize in Classics and has dealings with the history teacher Dunstan Ramsay. On graduation, he continues his education at Oxford.

In England he meets Colonel Copplestone, a friend of his father's, and is recruited to keep a lookout for any suspicious characters — Europe is on the brink of war and His Majesty's government could always use an extra spy. He also meets Tancred Saraceni, one of Europe's finest art connoisseurs, who is greatly taken with Francis's talent and offers him insight into the painting styles of the Renaissance. Francis's training under Tancred is interrupted, however, when he discovers his beloved cousin Ismay Glasson is pregnant — he slept with her once and is readily persuaded he is the father. He returns to England and marries her, the problem being she loves the no-good Charlie Fremantle, and the baby truthfully belongs to him; she has only married Francis for the convenience of his wealth — he has inherited a sizeable fortune from his late grandfather. Refusing to be trapped by Ismay's machinations, Francis abandons the scene and swears off any future marriage partner.

It is at this time that he is recruited by Colonel Copplestone to travel to Schloss Dusterstein in Bavaria, where he remains for most of the war. There he works under Tancred Saraceni, who has been hired to restore the Countess von Ingelheim's priceless collection that consists of various old master paintings. In actual fact, Tancred instructs Francis in the art of forgery, teaching him the paints to use, how to deploy the right brushstroke, and how to achieve the tiny cracks (the *craquelure*) that every fine painting develops over time. Eventually Francis proves so adept at these techniques that he not only proves a masterly forgery a fake when called upon by several experts to do so, but produces several forgeries of his own that are assumed to be by the hand of an unknown Renaissance genius. One such painting, *The Marriage at Cana*, is a symbolic treatment of his own life and is so successful that Tancred speaks of it as follows:

> Your picture is by no means an exercise in a past manner; those things always betray a certain want of real energy, and this has plenty of energy, the unmistakable impression of here and now. Something unquestionably from the Mothers. Reality of artistic creation, in fact. You have found a reality that is not part of the chronological present. Your here and now are not part of our time. You seem not to be trapped, as most of us are, in the psychological world of today. I hate such philosophical pomposities, but your immanence is not tainted by the calendar. One cannot predict with certainty, but this should wear well.

Francis's success dooms him, however, to abandon his painting in the post-war period: if he were to keep painting, his deceptions of the past would be discovered. He therefore has to content himself with amassing art, a practice he follows to the end of his days, hence the enormous collection that he leaves behind.

The peculiar coincidence was that, even as Davies was centring his story around Darcourt's efforts to write the life of Francis Cornish, he himself was the subject of a biography. Before this date several people were either writing or had written about Davies — Elspeth Cameron Buitenhuis, journalist June Callwood, and Michael Peterman are three examples — but none had ventured on a study of Davies's life in all its aspects. When Judith Skelton Grant approached him with her idea for the project, he possibly did not foresee how deeply she would probe his essentials. The project would continue for many years and would lead Grant to read many volumes of manuscripts, to travel to the places where Davies had lived, to interview his friends, colleagues, and family members as well as the grand old man himself — the latter on some seventy occasions. Although Grant was as diplomatic as she was meticulous, Davies sometimes resented her cross-examinations, even as he learned valuable lessons from her investigative methods.

"So, what's it like," a friend asked him over supper, "to be the subject of a biography?"

"It's hellish, to tell you the truth. No man with any self-respect should turn himself inside out to accommodate the ambitions of a would-be Boswell. Judith has asked to see my diaries! She has no bowels of compassion."

"I suppose she wishes to see you in all your dimensions."

"Of course she does. It makes good copy. But why would anyone consent to have his demonic side exposed, or the maggoty-headed jackass within?"

"She is very thorough."

"That too is a problem. I fear she'll spill all the details, both magnificent and trivial, and wind up mixing them all together. Besides, it's a senseless exercise."

"Oh? Why's that?"

"Because no matter how hard a biographer works, she can't plumb the person within. The inner self is as slippery as an eel, and the scholar's endless reading and footnotes are not the net to catch this trickster."

"So how can people know you?"

"I thought that was obvious: by reading my novels!"

What's Bred in the Bone was published in 1985. Once again, the reviews were glowing. Some critics complained that the plot was contrived and, again, that Davies was a die-hard elitist, but most reviewers appreciated the novel's many strengths, its description of early Canada, its parade of characters, the attention paid to the technical aspects of painting, and the attempt to reflect the artist's commitment to the act of discovery, not to mention a fascinating plot. Davies's handling of a central theme, too, that art is ultimately an act of deception but one that reveals crucial, universal truths, was consummately handled.

Davies's reputation as a front rank writer was brought home to him again by strong, international reviews, the translation of his books into a multitude of languages, and the impressive number of sales he registered. He had also been invited as a special guest to the 48th International PEN Congress, and had won the National Award from the Banff Centre School of Fine Arts. The greatest indication of his success, however, fell from the blue. In the early fall of 1986, as he was touring Sweden as a matter of coincidence, he learned that he had been shortlisted for that year's Nobel Prize in Literature — the most prestigious international award in literature. And Davies's cup was suddenly overflowing. Leaving Sweden, with the winner of the Nobel Prize to be determined in mid-October, Davies and Brenda stopped off in London. That was when he discovered that *What's Bred in the Bone* had been nominated for the Booker Prize, the most coveted award for literature in the English-speaking world.

"You must be so excited," Brenda told him when he sat down for breakfast in their London flat — one they owned on a time-share basis. It was the night after he had learned of this second nomination.

"These damned prizes have stuffed my pillow with thorns. I didn't sleep a wink. The more I try to cast them from my mind, the more they attack me and prod me awake."

"They would be huge feathers in your cap."

"I'm not even sure I want them, or deserve them for that matter."

"That's the Presbyterian leaking out."

"Unquestionably. Once a Calvinist always a Calvinist — even if I've switched to the Anglican perspective. But at the same time I yearn for these prizes more than I can say, like Atalanta hankering after those golden apples. No, more like Narcissus falling in love with his own reflection."

"Well you'd better tear yourself away from the mirror, Narcissus. There are dozens of journalists who want a piece of your glory."

"They won't let an old man finish his Corn Flakes?"

The results came in the following month. Davies discovered that the Booker had been won by Kingsley Amis — with himself as runner up. The Nobel, too, eluded him: it fell to Wole Soyinka, the Nigerian poet and playwright. Davies was crestfallen to be sure, but at least he could sleep soundly at night. And the best remedy for disappointment, he knew, was work: writer's work.

Davies's attraction to a novel that would unfold around an opera had been triggered back in 1981 when he collaborated with Derek Holman on *Dr. Canon's Cure*. At the same time he wished to resolve his characters' stories in *The Rebel Angels* and *What's Bred in the Bone*. The result is a complicated tale that Davies started writing in January 1987.

The Lyre of Orpheus again involves characters from the previous two novels: Maria, Arthur, and Simon Darcourt. This time around, Arthur has decided to commission a young composer,

Hulda Schnakenburg ("Schnak"), to complete an opera (*Arthur of Britain*) left unfinished by E.T.A. Hoffman, a nineteenth-century German composer and writer, as part of her thesis in composition. The world-renowned musicologist and conductor, Dr. Gunilla Dahl-Soot, is hired to supervise the talented, but philistine Schnak, and through a mix of domination and sexual seduction, leads her student to turn Hoffman's fragmentary score into a finished product that the composer could have written.

To complement these efforts, the producer Geraint Powell is brought on board to organize the singers, and arrange the opera's staging and set design. Mimicking unconsciously King Arthur's story — the good king is cuckolded by his right-hand man Lancelot — Geraint fathers a child on Maria when the latter somehow mistakes him for her lawful husband. Arthur is eventually brought to see that this unwelcome development is an instance of reality being shaped by art/mythology.

Simon Darcourt lends a helping hand. He writes a libretto for the opera, one consistent with the period's requirements, even as he presses on with his biography of Francis Cornish. In fact, he finally gets to the root of Francis's career as a forger when he stumbles on some of Francis's drawings that the Countess von Ingelheim's daughter has used to advertise a line of cosmetics.

Finally, the ghost of E.T.A. Hoffman appears intermittently — the novel's title is derived from his criticism of Beethoven's Fifth Symphony, "The lyre of Orpheus opens the door of the underworld." It turns out Hoffman's spirit has been languishing in limbo and, his interest piqued by these efforts to finish his opera, he comments now and then on the proceedings.

The opera's actual performance takes place, and Davies brings to bear his vast knowledge of the Victorian stage and set design. The description is powerful, as the following passage illustrates:

It had been the suggestion of Waldo Harris, not to the casual eye an imaginative man, that for this scene the forty-foot depth of the stage should be increased by opening the huge sliding doors to the storage rooms, and beyond them into the workshops, so that in the end a vista of a hundred feet could be attained. Not a great depth, surely, but with the aid of perspective painting it could be made to seem limitless. And ... when first Queen Guenevere was seen, at the farthest distance, on her black steed, it was not Donalda Roche, a woman of operatic sturdiness of figure, but a child of six, mounted on a pony no bigger than a St. Bernard. At a point perhaps sixty feet from the footlights the midget Guenevere rounded a grove of trees to be replaced by a larger child, mounted on a larger pony, led by a larger page. This Guenevere, forty feet from the footlights, disappeared for a moment in May blossom and it was Donalda Roche from the onward, on a black horse of normal stature. Behind her, pages led two magnificent white goats with gilded horns. Waldo and Dulchy had played with this illusion, and refined it, until it changed from a simple trick of perspective into a thing of beauty.

The novel, and trilogy, end on the brightest of notes. "Schnak" receives her doctorate, and has been polished by Soot into a more civilized person. Simon publishes his biography of Francis Cornish and, instead of dashing the man's reputation, enables him to receive posthumous recognition as a consummate artist in his own right. Arthur has forgiven his wife and accepts their baby as his own progeny, with the acquiescence of Geraint Powell. And E.T.A. Hoffman's afflicted ghost is finally laid to rest. As is always the case in Davies's estimate, art purifies the collective soul at large.

"I've finished it," Brenda announced, appearing in her husband's study at Windhover and placing the typescript for *The Lyre of Orpheus* on his desk.

"Well?" Davies asked, from his position by the window. He was standing beneath a beam of oak that had been taken from the house in Wales where his father had been born. "Is it any good, or have I wasted my time?"

"It amazes me," Brenda chuckled, "how even after you've been nominated for the Booker and the Nobel Prize, you still think of yourself as a second-rate hack."

"That's the doing of my unhappy childhood. But tell me what you think."

"I think it's a marvellous conclusion to the Cornish Trilogy. Your description of the staging of *Arthur of Britain* literally took my breath away. You've achieved something remarkable and ..."

"And? Come on, spit it out."

"Well, as in your other books, you make the convincing argument that art really matters, that music, good writing, and visual splendours redeem us. If I were a scientist or, worse, an accountant, and were to read the trilogy in one fell swoop, I think I'd feel my life was impoverished, a mere shadow of what it ought to be."

"So I've earned my supper, have I?"

"And a sumptious dessert."

The Lyre of Orpheus appeared in bookstores in 1988. It received the usual critical acclaim and sold exceptionally well in

Canada, England, and the U.S. Far from tiring of the old man, his fans could not drink their fill of his wisdom.

Although he was seventy-five and creaky at the knees, Davies roamed ceaselessly to promote his novels. Wherever he was scheduled to appear, the venue was invariably standing-room-only. And the same was true when Davies delivered speeches on a multitude of themes — painting, music, science fiction, morality in literature, and writing in the age of technology, to give but a few examples of his interests.

"Do you realize you've sold close to 600,000 of your books in the United States?" his U.S. publisher informed him at a restaurant in downtown New York City.

"Is that so remarkable?" Davies asked, "*The Godfather* has sold millions and millions."

"It is for a writer of literary fiction. If anyone has earned his retirement, it's you."

"Retirement!" Davies thundered, half rising to his feet. "That's the dirtiest insult you could fling my way. I'll have you know I'll only retire when I'm buried six feet under!"

Of course, he was taking notes for yet another book.

Davies in his study at Windhover, summer 1988.
Photo courtesy of Brian Willer Photography.

9

The Final Frontier

One's family is made up of supporting players in one's personal drama. One never supposes that they starred in some possibly gaudy and certainly deeply felt show of their own.
(*Murther and Walking Spirits*)

The inert mind is a greater danger than the inert body, for it overlays and stifles the desire to live.
(*The Cunning Man*)

Death, though people prate about its universality, is doubtless individual in the way it comes to everyone.
(*What's Bred in the Bone*)

Funerals are among the few ceremonials left
to us, and we assume our roles almost without
thinking.

(*The Manticore*)

This is the Great Theatre of Life. Admission is
free but the taxation is mortal. You come when
you can, and leave when you must. The show is
continuous. Good night.

(*The Cunning Man*)

"So we've reached the final chapter, have we, Maimas?"

"All human enterprise must reach an end, Zadkiel."

"Old age must be ghastly, what with the loss of your strength and the proximity of the dark."

"It is no joke for many, old man, but Robertson was determined to keep pushing to the very end, savouring the coffee grinds at cup's bottom. There is an art to everything, as he himself knew well, including the act of leaving the stage."

"So he continued to write?"

"To the last grain of sand in his life's hourglass. Because he knew that was the ticket, you see."

"To a life well-lived."

"And to an enduring reputation."

"It's very sad, the human condition."

"And a source of glory, dear Zadkiel, to which we angels can never aspire."

"What's he working on now?" Davies's youngest daughter Rosamond asked her mother, nodding at Davies who was sitting at the desk in his Windhover office. It was late December 1990 and, to escape the world's incessant talk about an impending war to liberate Kuwait from Iraq, Rosamond was staying with her parents for Christmas.

"He's just finishing up another novel. Where's Cecilia?" Brenda asked, referring to her youngest granddaughter.

"She's downstairs — she's too frightened to approach his study because she knows he gets grumpy if there's noise when he's working. But why's he writing another novel? He's already written nine of them and, together with his other stuff, you'd think he'd have run out of things to say."

"Not your father. And this novel touches on something new. He said it's an elaborate ghost story."

"That sounds like vintage Daddy. He loves talking about ghosts. Just last night he frightened Cecilia with one of his tales. Of course she immediately asked for another. But I don't understand why he's working so hard. Doesn't he want to have any time to relax?"

"I'll tell you why," Davies boomed from inside his office. "In the words of my mother, it's better to bust out than rust out! There's your explanation!"

Murther and Walking Spirits starts with the death of newspaperman Connor "Gil" Gilmartin, who is murdered by his colleague Randal Allard Going (the "Sniffer"), whom he has caught red-handed having sex with his wife, Esme. Instead of dying normally, Gil feels his spirit detach from his body and he is now wandering the world in the guise of a ghost, able to absorb the events around him, but unable to affect the physical realm. Furious that he has been deprived of his life, he hankers for vengeance against his killer, even as he admires his wife's self-control and ability to act the grieving, injured widow.

In an effort to inflict harm on the Sniffer, he follows him to a movie theatre — the Toronto Film Festival is in full swing and, as a theatre critic, the Sniffer is intent on watching and reporting on a series of rare old films. When the lights dim and the projector comes to life, however, there is an otherworldly intrusion: instead of viewing the film that the rest of the audience sees, Gil's ghost is confronted with the movie version of his own family's history.

A complicated narrative ensues, involving the many characters from Davies's complex family tree. There is his mother's side — the Loyalists fleeing the American Revolution, as well as the Highland Scots who lost their farms and were shipped off to the James Bay region. Florence's father, too, stages a lengthy appearance, complete with his morphine addiction, and Florence herself deceives her husband by shaving years off her real age. Rupert's side receives the same lavish treatment. Gil sees the story of his relative Thomas Gilmartin unfold — he is a wandering wool salesman who brings John Wesley's Methodism to the Welsh hinterlands. He also views the success of his grandfather's tailor business, its subsequent collapse, and, two generations on, the migration of his father to Canadian shores. In other words, Davies sets his entire family history on display, more often than not adhering closely to the many tales he had heard in his youth, and to the family memoir Rupert had composed and published in 1962, *Far-Off Fields.*

When these films finally reach a decisive end — they close with the message "Nothing is finished till all is finished" —

Gil continues to follow his wife and the Sniffer. Much to his satisfaction, he overhears Esme tell Going that she is pregnant and the baby must be Gil's, not his. When Going expresses surprise that she continued sleeping with her husband, even as she caroused with him, Esme announces that of course she continued to have sex with Gil, because she was very fond of him. Gil's spirit exclaims as follows:

> Oh, Esme, you can't believe how overjoyed I am to hear you say that! My dear, dear wife, how I love you at this moment! And — and Anna, and Elizabeth and Janet and Malvina and Rhodri [all relatives of his] — yes, and I suppose the McOrmishes, will all, in some measure, live on. I see the continuance of life as I never did while I was a part of it.

The Sniffer, too, receives his comeuppance. When he and Esme attend a seance, Gil sings in his murderer's ears the First World War song "The Bells of Hell Go Ting-a-ling-a-ling for You and Not for Me." Going immediately stands and visits St. Michael's College (at the University of Toronto) where he confesses his crime to Father Boyle but receives no absolution in return. On the advice of the priest, however, he does reveal his guilt to Hugh McWearie, Gil's colleague and trusted friend, who dismisses the Sniffer with the following observation:

> "Suppose I turn you in: you'd probably be charged with manslaughter, because your act was not premeditated; you'd get something like three years, and you'd be out long before that, because

these days the dice are heavily loaded in favour of
the murderer. It's a hot dinner for the wrongdoer,
and cold potatoes for the wronged person. And
after prison I suppose you'd think of yourself as a
man who'd paid his debt. So I'm not doing you a
great favour in letting you walk out of this room
a free man, because a free man is precisely what
you'll never be."

Murther and Walking Spirits was published in March 1991.
The reading public, together with most literary critics, even
ones who were admirers of Davies, were not quite sure what
to make of the novel. The general feeling was that the plot was
too complex — especially the narrative device of the films —
and that, while Davies went to great lengths to bare his family's
history honestly and with a copiousness of detail, the overall
emotional level was decidedly cool. The public's lackadaisical
response translated into faltering sales.

Not that Davies cared. He had written the novel partly
because he wished to get to the bottom of his Canadian identity
and expose the bedrock upon which it rested, and partly because
he felt he ought to commemorate his relatives, not only because
they had shaped him, but because they had engaged in the "Hero
Struggle" and fought against the odds till their last dying breath.
The sales and poor reviews did not trouble Brenda, either. For
the first time, Davies added a dedication to one of his books and
it read, "For Brenda."

"You didn't have to, Rob. I know the book belongs to your
readers and —"

"We have been married fifty years, Pink. I couldn't have
achieved my success in your absence. You have made our house

what it is and have borne the brunt of raising our children. But it's more than that. I'm thinking of our conversations. Through the entirety of our fifty years together, I have always had a fascinating conversation partner."

"So you stand by what you told me when you proposed to me, fifty years ago? That you were marrying me not so much as a lover, but as a friend?"

"I wouldn't change a single word of that assertion."

If the reception of *Murther and Walking Spirits* proved disappointing, Davies was heartened by an unexpected bit of theatrical success. In 1992 the assistant director of the Stratford Festival, Elliott Hayes, had adapted Davies's *World of Wonders* for the stage. Audiences were delighted with the show and the critics were appreciative.

Hayes had done such an impressive job, in fact, that he managed to attract Hollywood's notice. As it turned out, the film rights for *Fifth Business* had been purchased back in 1976 and had been floating around Hollywood for over fifteen years. Directors and producers were impressed with Davies's writings, but were not quite sure that his complex storylines could be translated onto the silver screen. With Hayes's successful treatment of *World of Wonders*, Hollywood's interest in Davies was renewed. Hayes flew down to Los Angeles and was soon working on a screenplay for *A Mixture of Frailties*. Unfortunately, a year into the project, tragedy struck from out of the blue.

"I just got off the phone with Richard Monette, Elliott's colleague at Stratford," Davies told Brenda, his face unnaturally pale. "It appears Elliott was killed by a drunken driver."

"Oh no!"

"It's a dreadful tragedy, of course."

"I suppose I shouldn't ask, but what will happen to the screenplay?"

"It's finished. Dead in the water."

"Are you sure? You don't think —"

"My novels will not be turned into films. Not within my lifetime, at least."

Davies consoled himself in his usual fashion: despite several setbacks with his health, a busy schedule of lecturing and readings, and the feeling that he was possibly yesterday's man, he was toiling away at yet another novel — his eleventh.

"Is it connected to *Murther and Walking Spirits*?" his editor, Elizabeth Sifton, asked him.

"I suppose so, Elizabeth. Like *Murther*, it is set in Toronto, and it will contain some of the same characters — Hugh McWearie, Esme Barron, and, in a minor role, Connor Gilmartin."

"Will you talk about his murder?"

"Yes, but minimally. It hardly has an effect on the plot. And I know what you're thinking."

"Oh?"

"You're worried because *Murther* didn't do so well, and here I am following the same barren path which will lead to bad sales and —"

"I hate to tell you this, Rob, but you're a lousy mind reader. I wasn't thinking any such thing. Instead I am only excited by the prospect of having yet another manuscript of yours in hand. The sooner the better."

Like *Murther and Walking Spirits*, *The Cunning Man* involves a sudden death in its opening pages. While officiating at the Good Friday service, Father Hobbes of the High Anglican church St. Aidan's suffers heart failure and dies on the spot. A long-time congregant of the church, Dr. Jonathan Hullah, describes the death to journalist Esme Barron and, in the process, ponders his own life story. The usual, labyrinthine narrative ensues — usual for Davies, at least. It turns out Dr. Hullah grew up in the northern Ontario town of Sioux Lookout where, in addition to the rational influences of his mine-owning father, he was saved by the Ojibwa medicine woman Mrs. Smoke. After opening his eyes to an approach that was at odds with the norms of western medicine, this mysterious woman revealed to him his totemic animal — the snake.

The effects of Mrs. Smoke's teachings affect Hullah through the course of his life. After passing through Colborne College (again, Upper Canada College) and studying medicine at the University of Toronto, he understands that his chosen field is not entirely a matter of science, but requires a less rational, more humanistic element if a doctor is going to prove successful when treating his patients. Indeed, the god Hermes's staff, the caduceus, with its two twisting snakes, not only stands in for Hullah's totemic animals but symbolizes his professional approach, as a philosophizing character named Jock explains:

> Once when Hermes walked abroad he came on two snakes fighting furiously. To make peace and establish balance, or reconciliation or whatever, he thrust his staff between the snakes and they crawled up it, still hissing, but this time in concord, and they have remained twined about the staff of the healer to this day. And what are the snakes? You could call them Knowledge and Wisdom.... Knowledge and Wisdom and they are not the same, because Knowledge is what you are taught, but

Wisdom is what you bring to it. Here's Jon,
he's right in the middle of it at this moment. He's being taught, and what is he being taught? Science, of course. Very fine, very
splendid, very indisputable until somebody
comes along with a new notion that squelch-
es the old one. But he is also bringing to it
the other snake, and we'll call it Humanism,
though that doesn't rule out the gods.

A combined scientist and humanist, Hullah becomes a
formidable, albeit unconventional, diagnostician — in short, a
"cunning man" — and wins a reputation for himself as a doctor
of last recourse, an expert whom patients visit when their regular
physicians have failed. His process of discovery consists of staring
at his patients, sniffing their orifices, listening attentively to their
stomachs' gurgles, smelling their breath, and engaging them in
long conversations.

After numerous incidents with his neighbours and clients,
Hullah gets to the bottom of Father Hobbes's death. It turns
out Charlie Iredale, a former schoolmate of Hullah's and Father
Hobbes's assistant, has heard Jesus speak to him in his sleep,
advising him to find a saint so that the city of Toronto can be
redeemed of its sins. To accomplish this quest, he explains to
Hullah, he had to arrange a saintly death for Father Hobbes, and
so he killed him with a poison-coated host.

The novel's principal idea is communicated at tale's end,
in a conversation between Jonathan and Esme, whom the former is still attracted to despite knowing she has killed her husband Connor.

"Do you think Gil *is* anywhere?" [Esme asks Hullah] "Or is death simply extinction?"

I think extinction is coming it a bit too strong. It's said energy is never lost, and there is a lot of energy in a human being, even an inferior one, and Gil certainly wasn't inferior."

"So where is that energy now?"

"If I knew that I would indeed be a Cunning Man. But of course you realize that what we're saying is wildly unscientific?"

"About the energy being somewhere, you mean?"

"About any suggestion that there is a plan, or an order, or a scheme of any kind in the Universe; no purposefulness in the evolutionary sequence whatever — not a particle. The scientific orthodoxy is that it all takes place by chance — even though it seems very odd that chance phenomena can build up systems of vast complexity. It is wholly against the law of entropy —"

"You've lost me."

"Don't worry. There is an alternative. And that's the notion of a Divine Drama.... The onward march of evolution. Astonishing, so far as it's gone, but we're probably only in Act Two of a five-act tragicomedy. We're probably a mere way station on the road to something finer than anything we can now conceive."

The Cunning Man contained elements of Davies's previous novels: there was the transition from small-town life to big-city practices (*Mixture of Frailties, Fifth Business, What's Bred in the Bone*), the tension between rationalism and faith/instinct (*Fifth Business, The Manticore, The Rebel Angels*), and a lone man's internal journey towards true wisdom (*Mixture of Frailties, Fifth Business, The Rebel Angels, The Lyre of Orpheus, Murther and Walking Spirits*). Davies was not repeating himself so much as exploring core beliefs from a different perspective.

Even as *The Cunning Man* was published in 1994, to further lukewarm reviews, another book important to Davies finally appeared on the scene: Judith Skelton Grant's biography *Robertson Davies: Man of Myth*. Twelve years in the making, meticulous in its approach and documentation, Skelton's book was a very fair, indeed a laudatory, treatment of Davies and his literary career. Davies himself was disdainful by this stage. In spite of the fact that he was working with Grant on other projects — they had published a collection of Davies's essays together and were in the process of compiling his early letters — he avoided discussing the book with his biographer.

"I don't understand your reaction to the book. Judith treats you handsomely," Brenda observed as Davies was preparing for a reading from *The Cunning Man* that evening.

"It took her long enough to finish the brute, didn't it? I'm tired of being got at. I'll bet she was hoping I would die in the meantime, and then she could capture all my life between two covers."

"She was hoping no such thing. Indeed, you should write her a note of thanks for all the work she has invested in you."

"She's received compensation, hasn't she? She has a hefty work of scholarship to her credit and —"

"Hang on a moment! You haven't even read her book, have you? The finished version, I mean."

"What would be the point? I know my own story."

Although Davies was past the age of eighty now, he felt he had a schedule to keep. At the behest of his publisher, he pushed hard to promote *The Cunning Man*, even as other projects vied for his attention. In London, again on a reading tour, he and Brenda were always on the move and, to their misfortune, contracted the flu. They were ill for many weeks.

"This is it, Pink. I'm on my last legs," Davies groaned from somewhere deep inside a mass of blankets.

"I've heard that before."

"No, I'm serious. I'm on the way out."

"Do you know how many times you've said the end is near? Through all your bouts of asthma and heart spasms, not to mention your insufferable indigestion, you've always maintained your appetite and vigour."

"This time it's different, Pink."

"That's enough defeatist talk from you!"

When the bug finally left his system, Davies was taking notes for another novel, despite his sorely weakened condition. His plan was to write about a man who travels across Canada, and possibly to connect this trip to themes he had pursued in his last two novels – a Toronto Trilogy, he was thinking. Unfortunately, even as he was gathering information (with some help from Jennifer, his middle daughter, who was acting as his secretary), he discovered he was scheduled for a long trip of his own.

In mid-November 1995, Davies suffered a serious stroke. Although he recovered partially, he had trouble engaging people in complex conversations, and composing simple notes was suddenly difficult. The man who had been a ready source of anecdotes and *bons mots* all his life was suddenly at a loss for words.

One night he was on his own in the Orangeville Hospital — Brenda had gone home for the evening and the nurse was busy with a different patient. That was when an old acquaintance came to visit. Opening his eyes, he saw standing at the foot of his bed the ghostly witch who had plagued him through the course of his childhood, never issuing a single word and always confronting him with a blood-sucking grin.

"You again," Davies murmured. "I haven't seen you in a long time."

The witch just looked at him, as gnarled and misshapen as always, and with that abiding look of out-and-out malevolence.

"I have learned a great deal since we last met," he continued with an effort. "I understand things are not always what they seem to be, and that you ghosts sometimes wish to frighten, but sometimes your goal is to inspire as well. It could be you showed yourself to me to prove there is another face to the world, and if this is so, I am in your debt."

The witch considered him evenly. By God she was ugly!

"I don't suppose you would consider being friends with me, would you?"

At these words the witch's expression changed, from one of seeming violence to one of ... open affection. She nodded affably and whispered words of comfort. At that moment a nurse appeared in the doorway and the apparition vanished.

Always terrified that he would "die stupid," that his soul would shrivel up while his body continued with its regular functions, Davies's fears were soon put to rest. On December 2, 1995 a second, devastating stroke struck home. Aware his life was quickly seeping away, Davies stared out the window of his hospital room to the distant, snow-glazed fields outside. He was thinking how much Canada had changed through the course of his lifetime. He was thinking how he had been formed by his ancestors, and he in turn would shape the succeeding generations. He was thinking, too, how as much as he had complained about the backwardness of Canada, he was Canadian through and through and the very shapelessness of Canada in his early youth had given him the opportunity to impress it with his stamp — just as it had left its stamp on him. He was thinking, too, as the last of his breath was being squeezed from his lungs, that he had barely wasted a minute of his eighty-plus years, that he had known love and raised a family and stretched himself and left a legacy behind — a great, fat legacy that legions of readers could subsist on for generations to come. And his last thought was, "All is finished."

Three days later Davies's funeral was held at Trinity College, where Davies had taught for over twenty years. Obituaries appeared in all the major publications of the English-speaking world, and various celebrities spoke at a memorial service a few days later. Further compilations of his essays and talks would be published down the road, and Davies's novels would become part of the Canadian literary canon. If a typical Canadian high school student were stopped at random and asked if the name "Robertson Davies" struck a bell, the answer would be near universal: "Robertson Davies, the bearded ogre, the one who was interested in magic, saints, and otherworldly stuff. Yeah, I know the guy."

And Davies's robust laughter would ring out from the grave.

Davies, as Samuel Marchbanks, on the cover of Liberty *magazine, April 1954. Photo by Walter Curtin.*

Epilogue

Elusive Voyager

"That's quite a story, Maimas. When you think of the world Davies was born into — small-town Ontario in 1913 — and how the world was his oyster at the time of his death, I have to admit his progress was astounding."

"It's fascinating, too, Zadkiel old man, how the human imagination can turn the dross of human disappointments into solid gold — an alchemical achievement Davies liked to dwell on."

"I'm not sure I follow you, my dear fellow."

"It should be clear by now, Zadkiel. Davies took his strict upraising, his early disappointments in love, his awful experiences in the backlands of Canada, his own confusion and insecurities, and, passing them through his writer's imagination, changed them into stories which, I'm willing to bet, will continue being read the next time we meet."

"All too true, Maimas. I suppose, though, that such fame is little compensation for the terrible price that all humans must pay. Death is so terribly unforgiving and —"

"Zadkiel, not another word. Close your eyes an instant and allow me to convey you to a place of my choosing."

"Yes, all right, but don't dilly-dally. I have other appointments to keep, you know, and I believe the night is well-advanced already."

"We're already here. You can open your eyes. There. Do you recognize the place?"

"Of course. I have been here many times. We're standing in the courtyard of Massey College."

"Yes. Now look into that window over to the right. Tell me what you see."

"There's a light on by a desk. And there's a big seated fellow who appears to be busy writing something. Wait. He's conscious of us — that's very odd, because people never know we're looking on ... Oh my goodness! Maimas, you sly devil, that's Robertson himself!"

"You mean, that's the ghost of Robertson, doing what he loves best. So you see, the story has a happy ending, one that's in keeping with our subject's convictions. And for the curious who have a nose for such things, well, they too can spy on Robertson if they're quick enough. But I see you're anxious to keep an appointment, Zadkiel, and I'll leave off there. Until we meet again."

"I hope it's sooner than we think."

Chronology of Robertson Davies (1913–1995)

Compiled by Nicholas Maes

Davies and His Times	Canada and the World
1790 Davies's Loyalist relatives (on his mother's side) leave the American colonies and travel north to Canada.	
1820 Deprived of their farms in Scotland, Davies's Highland forebears (again on his mother's side) arrive in Canada, in the James Bay region. They walk south to Ontario.	
	1869 The Hudson's Bay Company sells Rupert's Land (consisting of modern-day Manitoba, most of Saskatchewan, southern Alberta, southern Nunavut, some parts of northern Ontario and Quebec) to the Canadian government.

Davies and His Times	*Canada and the World*
	The Eaton family opens its first department store in downtown Toronto.
1870 Florence McKay (Davies's mother) is born in the village of Langford, Ontario.	
	1875 Canada's first organized hockey league game is played on Victoria Rink in Montreal, Quebec.
	1876 Alexander Graham Bell completes the first long-distance telephone call, between Brantford and Paris, Ontario.
1879 Rupert Davies (Davies's father) is in born in Welshpool, Wales.	
	1885 The Canadian Pacific Railway system across Canada is completed, providing rapid transportation across the continent.
	Louis Riel leads the Northwest Rebellion, the uprising of the Métis people against the Dominion of Canada. It is crushed and Riel is hanged. The new Canadian Pacific Railway

Davies and His Times	*Canada and the World*
	plays a large role in the rapid deployment of federal forces.
1890 Walter Davies (Davies's grandfather) faces a downturn in his tailoring business and teeters on the verge of bankruptcy.	
	1891 The Massey Manufacturing Company merges with A. Harris and Son to become the world's largest manufacturer of agricultural machinery.
1894 Rupert Davies (aged fifteen) and his brother Percy immigrate to Canada. They settle in Brantford, Ontario. The rest of the family joins them one year later.	
1896 Rupert begins his apprenticeship as a junior printer in Brantford.	**1896** Liberal leader Wilfrid Laurier becomes Canada's seventh prime minister (and the first of French-Canadian descent). He quickly introduces an "open-door" policy on immigration to encourage population expansion in the new western provinces. From 1901 to 1913, 2.7 million people will arrive on Canada's shores.
	1898 Gold fever attracts thousands of

Davies and His Times	*Canada and the World*
	prospectors to the Klondike in Canada's Yukon region.
	1899 The second Boer War starts. This will be a protracted war that pits soldiers from the various dominions of the British Empire against the Dutch Boers of South Africa. In France, Captain Alfred Dreyfus is wrongly accused and hastily convicted of treason. His situation provokes a frenzied national debate.
1900 Rupert passes his exams for the Typographical Union. He works in New York City and Toronto, but returns to Brantford because he misses his family.	
1901 Rupert Davies falls in love with Florence McKay and marries her after a brief courtship of six months. He is under the impression that she is several years younger than she actually is, and their marriage will suffer because of this deception.	**1901** Queen Victoria, the longest reigning British monarch, dies at the age of 81. Her son, Prince Edward, assumes the throne, ruling as Edward VII. Guglielmo Marconi receives the first transatlantic signal at Signal Hill, St. John's, Newfoundland.
1902 Frederic Rupert Davies is born, the eldest of Davies's brothers.	

Davies and His Times

1903
Arthur Llewelyn Davies is born, Davies's second brother.

1907
Rupert moves his family to Thamesville where he takes charge of the local paper, the *Thamesville Herald*. Thamesville will serve as Deptford in Davies's famous Deptford Trilogy.

Canada and the World

1903
Ford Motor Company is established by Henry Ford and his partners.

The Wright brothers put into flight the world's first plane with a petrol engine at Kitty Hawk, North Carolina.

1905
Alberta and Saskatchewan join the Canadian Confederation. The Great Toronto Fire destroys a large part of the city's downtown area — 104 buildings in total.

Einstein publishes his famous paper on special relativity.

1906
The Ouimetoscope opens in Montreal. It is the first Canadian theatre dedicated exclusively to the viewing of movies. It has a thousand seats and features a six-piece orchestra.

Davies and His Times

1908
Rupert purchases the first of his newspapers, the *Thamesville Herald*.

Canada and the World

1908
Henry Ford introduces his Ford Model T — a car that will sell by the hundreds of thousands.

L.M. Montgomery's *Anne of Green Gables* is published. It will quickly become a treasured Canadian classic.

1910
In an effort to satisfy British requests for funding from Canada (and other colonies) to build more ships for the British navy, Prime Minister Laurier passes the Naval Service Bill. It allows for the construction of a Canadian navy, under Canadian control, but offers the loan of such a force to Britain in times of war.

1911
Wilfrid Laurier promotes Reciprocity with the U.S. — or the reciprocal elimination of tariffs on various American and Canadian products. The proposal stirs huge controversy. Laurier decides to call an election and is roundly defeated by Conservative politician Robert Borden.

1912
Humorist Stephen Leacock's *Sunshine Sketches of a Little Town* is published.

Davies and His Times	*Canada and the World*

Canada and the World

Roald Amundsen reaches the South Pole, beating the English expeditionary party led by Robert Scott.

1913

Davies and His Times

William Robertson Davies is born on August 28. He is named after his father's brother, William Robertson, who died two years earlier of tuberculosis.

1913

Over four hundred thousand immigrants arrive in Canada in this year — a record number.

1914

Serbian Nationalist Gavril Princip assassinates Archduke Ferdinand and his wife in Sarajevo. Within two months of this event France, England, and Russia are at war with Austria-Hungary and Germany. The First World War has begun. England's declaration of war on Germany automatically involves Canada in the war. Large numbers of Canadian volunteers rush to sign up.

1915

Canadians are involved in their first significant battle at Ypres in Belgium. Despite their poor armaments (the Ross rifle) and the Germans' use of gas, they fight capably.

John McRae writes his famous poem "In Flanders Fields."

Davies and His Times

Canada and the World

The passenger ship *Lusitania* is sunk by German U-boats off the coast of Ireland.

1916
The French launch the Battle of Verdun. The ten-month battle will claim over a million casualties. In July, the English initiate the Battle of the Somme; it will also result in well over a million casualties (24,000 of these will be Canadian).

1917
U.S. president Woodrow Wilson publishes his Fourteen Points that argue for "Peace without victory" in Europe. Three months later, the United States enters the war on the side of Britain and its allies.

Canadian forces, under the brilliant leadership of Arthur Currie, capture Vimy Ridge.

The Conscription Crisis in Canada leads PM Robert Borden to introduce the Military Service Act, which stipulates military service is compulsory for males between the ages of twenty and forty-five. Borden also calls a federal election, even as he passes the Wartime Elections Act that grants the right to vote to female relatives of soldiers.

Davies and His Times	*Canada and the World*
	In November, Communist forces seize control of the Russian government. The tsar and his family are arrested and subsequently executed.
	1918 The First World War ends with the signing of an armistice on November 11.
1919 Rupert sells the *Thamesville Herald* and buys the larger *Renfrew Mercury*. He moves the family to Renfrew, Ontario. Davies will later excoriate this town, which will appear as Blairlogie in his novel *What's Bred in the Bone*. Davies starts his formal schooling at Renfrew's Central School. He becomes a voluminous reader.	**1919** The Versailles Treaty redraws the borders of Central Europe and the Middle East. It also creates the League of Nations, an international forum for the resolution of hostilities through negotiation and collective security. Finally, it imposes severe penalties on Germany for its involvement in the First World War. The Spanish flu kills between 20 and 100 million people worldwide. Fifty thousand Canadians die because of this disease. The Royal Northwest Mounted Police bring the Winnipeg General Strike to an end.
1921 Davies is transferred to the North Ward School. He is bullied and hates this institution.	**1921** Liberal Mackenzie King is elected prime minister of Canada.

Davies and His Times	*Canada and the World*
	Adolf Hitler becomes the leader of the German Workers' Party and changes its name to the Nationalist Socialist German Workers Party (NSDAP, or Nazis, for short).
1922 Davies has his first newspaper article published in the *Renfrew Mercury*. It is the first of thousands that he will publish in his career as a journalist, reviewer, and editor.	**1922** James Joyce's landmark novel *Ulysses* is published in Paris. Egyptologist Howard Carter discovers the tomb of Egyptian pharaoh Tutankhamen.
	Joseph Stalin is appointed general secretary of the Soviet Communist Party.
	1923 Kemal Ataturk declares Turkey a secular republic.
	Frederick Banting and J.J.R. MacLeod are awarded the Nobel Prize for the discovery of insulin. Banting shares his prize with Charles Best, his assistant.
	Adolf Hitler stages his Beer Hall Putsch in Munich, fails in his objectives, and is arrested.
	Canada passes the Chinese Exclusion Act, banning all Chinese (except students, diplomats, and merchants) from entering the country.

Davies and His Times

1924
Rupert travels to Europe with a group of Canadian editors. Davies accompanies him and has his first taste of England. He also tours the battlefields of the First World War.

1925
The American magician Harry Blackstone visits Renfrew. Davies is enthralled and begins his lifelong interest in magic.

Rupert purchases the *Daily British Whig* (a Kingston paper) and moves his family to Kingston. Davies attends the local junior high school, the Kingston Collegiate Institute.

1926
Rupert purchases Kingston's second paper, the *Kingston Daily Standard*, and amalgamates it with the *Daily British Whig* to produce the *Kingston Whig-Standard*.

1927
The renowned D'Oyly Carte's production of Gilbert and Sullivan's *Mikado* comes to Toronto. Davies catches the show and decides upon a career in the world of theatre.

Canada and the World

1925
Biology teacher John Scopes is arrested in Dayton, Tennessee for teaching Charles Darwin's Theory of Evolution.

1926
World-renowned magician and escapologist Harry Houdini dies of peritonitis after being punched in the stomach by a McGill University student.

1927
Charles Lindbergh is the first pilot to fly solo, non-stop across the Atlantic, from New York City to Paris.

The Jazz Singer — the first feature-length movie with a

Davies and His Times	*Canada and the World*

1928–32:
Davies attends Canada's foremost private school, Upper Canada College in Toronto. It will figure in a number of his novels in the guise of Colborne College. He contributes to the school newspaper (thereby attracting the notice of *Saturday Night*'s editor B.K. Sandwell) and participates in numerous plays (Shakespeare and Gilbert and Sullivan).

He trains himself to speak with a mid-Atlantic accent and dresses flamboyantly. While he is gifted in the Humanities, he is a very poor student of mathematics.

1932
Davies graduates from Upper Canada College in the spring, but with insufficient high school credits (he has failed mathematics). This poor performance means he cannot enter university.

Rupert takes Davies to Wales that summer where he purchases an estate (Fronfraith Hall). Through his connections, Rupert manages to get Davies admitted into Queen's University as a special student, with the proviso he will not receive his B.A. on graduation.

soundtrack — opens and proves a great success. It revolutionizes the movie industry.

1929
The U.S. stock market crashes on Thursday, October 24 and leads to the onset of the Great Depression. The world economy will be affected for ten years.

Britain's Privy Council announces that women are persons and therefore eligible to run for public office.

1930
Conservative leader R.B. Bennett becomes prime minister.

1931
The Statute of Westminster renders Canada completely self-governing and bound by no laws other than its own.

Davies and His Times

1932–33
Davies is enrolled in an Honours English program at Queen's University. He is better read than any other student and creates a stir with his wit and learning.

1933
In the fall, Davies stages a production of *Alice in Wonderland*. His efforts attract the notice of Mrs. Harriet Sweezey, who invites him to direct a version of the *Importance of Being Earnest* at her lavish country estate.

Davies becomes interested in the writings of psychologist Havelock Ellis, a pioneer in the study of human sexual relationships.

1934
At the very start of the year Davies meets Eleanor Sweezey, Mrs. Harriet Sweezey's eighteen-year-old daughter. Davies falls in love with her.

Davies joins his father in Wales that summer. He applies to Balliol College (part of Oxford University) for admission into the B.A. program.

Davies stages a version of Sophocles' *Oedipus the King*. It is a gory production and attracts a record crowd.

Canada and the World

1933
Adolf Hitler is appointed the Reich Chancellor of Germany by the country's president, Paul von Hindenburg. Three weeks after his rise to power, the German parliament building is destroyed through arson, triggering the Reichstag Fire Decree, which deprives German citizens of basic civil liberties.

1934
The Red Army of the Chinese Communist Party embarks on its Long March to evade the forces under the leadership of Chiang Kai-shek. Communist official Mao Zedong starts his ascent to power.

Hitler liquidates his political rivals in act of violence that will become known as the Night of the Long Knives.

Davies and His Times

1935

Davies graduates from Queen's, but receives no degree. He discovers late that summer that he has been accepted into Balliol. Before leaving for England, he proposes to Eleanor, but she is reluctant to marry him. She agrees to reconsider his offer down the road.

Davies sails for England and takes up residence in Balliol College. He starts preparing for examinations in Latin and Anglo-Saxon. He becomes a member of the prestigious OUDS (Oxford University Drama Society).

He writes to Eleanor every day.

1936

Disaster strikes when Davies fails his examinations in Latin and Anglo-Saxon.

He invites Eleanor to join him in Wales for the summer break, but she refuses. Davies writes her several stinging letters. She then ends their relationship.

Davies falls into tailspin. On the advice of his former psychology professor, Davies consults one of England's top-ranked

Canada and the World

1935

Mackenzie King becomes the prime minister of Canada for the second time.

Hitler institutes the infamous Nuremberg Laws, which deprive Germany's Jews of their German citizenship and legal rights.

1936

The Canadian Broadcasting Corporation is established.

Adolf Hitler reoccupies the Rhineland, in open violation of the Versailles Treaty. He also dispatches German troops to participate on the side of General Franco's fascist forces in Spain, where civil war has erupted.

Davies and His Times

psychiatrists, Dr. Gillespie, who
introduces him to the writings of
Sigmund Freud.

Back at Oxford, Davies's program
is adjusted: he is now pursuing
the less prestigious B.Litt. (a
research degree).

1937
Davies decides upon his
thesis subject for his B.Litt.:
Shakespeare's boy actors.

In the course of working on a
play for OUDS, Davies meets
Brenda Newbold for the first
time, an Australian who is the
stage manager for the Old Vic
Theatre in London.

1938
Davies completes his thesis.
He passes his oral examination
with flying colours and is urged
to get his thesis published.
He graduates and receives his
B.Litt.

Davies moves to London and
seeks work as an actor.

1939
Shakespeare's Boy Actors is published. It draws some positive
comments.

Canada and the World

1938
At the Munich Conference, British
prime minister Chamberlain and
French president Daladier agree
to Hitler's secessionist claims to
Czechoslovakia's Sudetenland.

Chamberlain declares that the
Munich Accord represents "Peace
for our time."

1939
In late August, Germany and
Russia sign the Molotov-
Ribbentrop Pact that grants Hitler
a free hand to invade Poland. On

Davies and His Times

Tyrone Guthrie, director of the
Old Vic Theatre, hires Davies
as an actor and the company
dramaturge. Davies reacquaints
himself with Brenda Newbold.

Davies makes several appearances
on the stage. He is advised by
theatre critic Lionel Hale to
try his hand as a playwright,
and warned to retire from the
stage before he is subjected to a
scathing review.

When war breaks out, Davies
proposes to Brenda and invites
her back to Canada. She accepts.

1940
Davies and Brenda get married
on February 2. They honeymoon
in Wales then sail to Canada,
where they live with Davies's
parents.

Brenda discovers that she is
pregnant.

Davies starts writing editorials
for the *Whig-Standard*. He is
soon contributing a thrice-
weekly column (entitled "Cap
and Bells") to the *Whig-Standard*
and *Peterborough Examiner*
(another paper owned by
Rupert). He writes under the
name Samuel Marchbanks.

Canada and the World

September 1 Germany invades
western Poland and, two days
later, Britain declares war on
Germany. Canada follows suit
one week later.

Canada's National Film Board is
established.

1940
Winston Churchill becomes
the prime minister of England.
German forces invade Holland,
France, and Belgium. The British
Expeditionary Force is boxed
in at Dunkirk and is evacuated
to England. In response to
the disaster at Dunkirk, the
Canadian Parliament passes the
National Resources Mobilization
Act, which requires all males
to register for military service
within Canada.

Davies and His Times	*Canada and the World*
These columns prove remarkably popular and he will continue them for thirteen years.	
Davies and Brenda move to Toronto. He is hired by B.K. Sandwell to become the literary editor for *Saturday Night*.	
The publishing house Clarke, Irwin and Co. commissions Davies to write an introductory book on Shakespeare for high school students.	
Davies's first daughter, Miranda, is born December 24.	

1941

The chief editor of the *Peterborough Examiner* dies unexpectedly in December. Rupert orders Davies to take over his job. Davies resigns from *Saturday Night*.

1941

After Nazi Germany invades Russia, the U.S.S.R. enters the war against Germany. Japan stages an attack on Pearl Harbor in Hawaii. The U.S. declares war on Japan and its allies, Germany and Italy.

1942

Davies moves his family to Peterborough, where he works as the editor of the *Peterborough Examiner*.

Shakespeare for Young Players appears.

Davies grows a beard during a lengthy bout with the flu and

1942

In the wake of the Japanese attack on Pearl Harbor, the Canadian authorities decide to intern all Japanese nationals as well as all Canadians of Japanese descent.

The Canadian raid on Dieppe is staged. It is an utter failure.

Davies and His Times	*Canada and the World*
decides to keep it; it will become his "badge" over the next fifty years. His journalistic regimen requires him to write twelve thousand words each week.	
Davies's second daughter, Jennifer, is born October 16.	
1943 Davies writes his first serious play, *The King Who Could Not Dream*. Tyrone Guthrie reacts positively and passes it on to English actor/director John Gielgud, but it is never produced.	**1943** Operation Husky — the assault on Sicily — is launched. Although it involves 2,310 Canadian casualties, it is successful and leads to the invasion of Italy.
1944 Davies writes six mini-plays for radio to promote interest in the Victorian Order of Nurses. He follows this up with another series of "playlets," this time to advertise Victory Loan Bonds. Neither campaign meets with much success.	**1944** On D-Day, June 6, a massive allied force storms the beaches of Normandy. Ten thousand Canadian troops land at Juno Beach. The Germans are steadily rolled back.
1945 Davies finishes writing his play *Hope Deferred*. It stirs no interest. Davies completes *A Jig for a Gypsy*, but this too gains him no recognition. Davies writes the one-act play *Overlaid*. He tries to convince the	**1945** U.S. president Franklin D. Roosevelt dies and is succeeded by Harry Truman. Four weeks later (May 8) Germany surrenders unconditionally, thereby ending the war in Europe. Nazi death camps, where millions of Jews were liquidated, are discovered.

Davies and His Times

CBC to stage it on radio as part of their *Stage* series, but they turn him down.

Canada and the World

Representatives from fifty nations meet in San Francisco and sign a charter that establishes the United Nations.

On August 6 an atomic bomb is dropped on Hiroshima. A second bomb is dropped on Nagasaki three days later. Japan surrenders unconditionally.

1946

Overlaid takes first prize in the Ottawa Drama League's Workshop competition.

Davies completes his comic one-act play, *Eros at Breakfast.*

1946

The Soviets refuse to relinquish their control over Eastern Europe. Winston Churchill declares that an "iron curtain has descended across the continent."

1947

Davies's third daughter, Rosamond, is born in April.

Clarke, Irwin agrees to publish a collection of Davies's Marchbanks columns. These appear under the title *The Diary of Samuel Marchbanks.* The book sells exceptionally well.

Eros at Breakfast takes first prize at the Ottawa Drama League Competition. It is performed by numerous amateur theatrical companies.

1947

The Truman Doctrine is proclaimed with a view to contain the global spread of communism.

India gains its independence from Britain.

The United Nations approves of Resolution 181. It signals an end to the British Mandate in Palestine and allows for the partition of Palestine into a Jewish half and an Arab one.

Davies and His Times	*Canada and the World*
Davies is diagnosed with Hodgkin's disease and undergoes intense radiation therapy. He and Brenda fear his life is in danger. He makes a full recovery.	
Rupert Davies becomes a member of the Canadian Senate. He divides the ownership of the *Peterborough Examiner* among his sons.	
1948 Davies's publisher, Clarke, Irwin, agrees to publish a collection of Davies's plays, including *Eros at Breakfast*.	**1948** Liberal leader Louis St. Laurent becomes prime minister of Canada
The Dominion Drama Festival, the country's foremost drama competition, chooses *Eros at Breakfast* as the Canadian submission to the Edinburgh Festival for 1949.	Through the Marshall Plan, the U.S. and Canada contribute over $13 billion in aid for the reconstruction of war-torn Europe.
Davies finishes writing his full-length play, *Fortune, My Foe*. It meets with some critical success.	Jewish leader David Ben-Gurion declares the independence of the nation of Israel. The Arab-Israeli War breaks out and ends with a Jewish victory.
Davies's mother Florence dies in December. He is sleeping in an adjoining room on the night of her death and is convinced her spirit visits him with murderous intent.	

Davies and His Times

1949

A second volume of Marchbanks columns is published by Clarke, Irwin, entitled *The Table Talk of Samuel Marchbanks.*

Eros at Breakfast fails to attract any notice at the Edinburgh Festival.

1950

Davies is asked to contribute to the Massey Commission (which is studying the state of the arts in Canada). His suggestions (as well as his colleagues') lead to the creation of the Stratford Festival. He also attracts the notice of Vincent Massey (the future governor general of Canada).

Frustrated that he has no control over the staging of his plays, Davies decides to write his next story as a novel. He begins taking notes for *Tempest-Tost.*

1951

Tempest-Tost is published — the first book in his Salterton Trilogy. It receives generally positive

Canada and the World

1949

Twelve western nations sign a mutual-defensive treaty and create the North Atlantic Treaty Organization (NATO).

Newfoundland and Labrador join Confederation

George Orwell's *1984* is published.

The Chinese Civil War ends and Mao Zedong declares the birth of the People's Republic of China.

1950

Communist North Korea attacks South Korea. U.S. forces under General Douglas MacArthur intervene on the side of South Korea. Canada supports this American initiative. The war will continue until 1953.

Davies and His Times	Canada and the World

reviews, and is picked up by American and English publishers.

1952
Davies sets to work on *Leaven of Malice*, his second novel.

1952
Elizabeth II is proclaimed queen of the United Kingdom following the death of her father, George VI.

Vincent Massey is sworn in as Canada's governor general.

Republican candidate Dwight Eisenhower defeats Adlai Stevenson in the U.S. presidential race.

1953
Davies is re-hired as the literary editor for *Saturday Night*.

He prepares a third volume in his Marchbanks series, entitled *Marchbanks' Almanack*. It is rejected by Clarke, Irwin.

1953
Watson and Crick discover the double-helix structure of the DNA molecule.

Edmund Hillary and Tenzing Norgay achieve the first successful ascent of Mount Everest.

1954
Davies's brother Fred is killed in a car accident on the island of Nassau, March 7.

Leaven of Malice appears. It receives generous reviews.

No longer convinced Freud's theories answer his own metaphysical inquiries, Davies starts reading the works Carl

1954
After a protracted war against the communist Viet Minh, France relinquishes all claims to its former colony Indochina. The territory is divided into North and South Vietnam.

The first Canadian subway system opens in Toronto.

Davies and His Times

Jung. He will study Jung's theories all his life, and they will figure prominently in his fiction.

1955
Davies writes a new play, *Hunting Stuart*. It is staged in the autumn and receives some warm reviews.

1956
Davies starts writing *A Mixture of Frailties*, the last volume in his Salterton Trilogy.

Canada and the World

1955
Rosa Parks refuses to cede her seat to a white passenger and is arrested in Montgomery, Alabama. The Civil Rights Movement catches fire.

1956
Hungarian protests against Communist rule lead to the intervention of Soviet forces.

Egyptian General Nasser nationalizes the Suez Canal, thereby provoking an Israeli attack on Egypt and the landing of joint French-British forces to protect the canal. Lester B. Pearson persuades the UN to ensure the creation and deployment of United Nations Emergency Forces (UNEF) to the region.

1957
Lester B. Pearson receives the Nobel Peace Prize for his intervention in the Suez Canal Crisis.

The U.S.S.R. launches the world's first space satellite, *Sputnik*.

Davies and His Times	*Canada and the World*
1958	**1958**
A Mixture of Frailties appears, receiving better reviews than his two previous volumes.	Conservative leader John Diefenbaker becomes prime minister of Canada.
Davies travels to New York City to consult with an astrologer. He is told that his most productive years are ahead of him still.	
Davies imagines a scene of one boy throwing a snowball at another — this will serve as the inspiration for his novel *Fifth Business*.	
New York publisher Alfred Knopf admires the reviews that Davies has written for *Saturday Night* and offers him a contract to write a collection of reviews (A *Voice from the Attic*) for his publishing house.	
1959	**1959**
New York producers are interested in a stage version of Davies's *Leaven of Malice*.	Fidel Castro overthrows the Batista government in Cuba. He soon aligns his country with the U.S.S.R.
1960	**1960**
Davies works with Tyrone Guthrie on the play version of *Leaven of Malice* — now entitled *Love and Libel.* It appears on the Toronto stage, and is taken on an American tour, with New York City as its final destination. It is an utter flop.	John F. Kennedy defeats Richard Nixon in the U.S. presidential race.

Davies and His Times

Davies is approached by Vincent Massey and offered the position of master of Massey College in Toronto — the College will be a residence for male graduate students and academics from a variety of backgrounds. He accepts.

Voices from the Attic appears.

1961–62
Davies cooperates closely with Massey in overseeing the construction of the college.

1962
Davies writes a one-act play, *A Masque for Mr. Punch*. It is performed in high schools across Canada.

1963
Massey College opens. Davies's responsibilities are many. He introduces a series of rituals that are based on Balliol's. He institutes the Christmas Gaudy — he will compose an annual ghost story for these occasions.

Canada and the World

1961
The New Democratic Party (NDP) is formed through the merger of the Canadian Labour Congress and the Co-operative Commonwealth Federation.

1962
U.S. reconnaissance planes detect Soviet missiles stationed in Cuba. Tensions erupt between the United States and the Soviet Union and set the world on the verge of a nuclear war. The Cuban Missile Crisis is defused only two weeks later.

1963
Liberal leader Lester B. Pearson becomes the prime minister of Canada.

President John F. Kennedy is assassinated by Lee Harvey Oswald in Dallas, Texas. He is succeeded by Vice-President Lyndon Johnson.

Davies and His Times

1966
Davies's second daughter, Jennifer, marries psychologist Colin Thomas Surridge.

Canada and the World

1964
The Beatles perform on *The Ed Sullivan Show*, their first live television performance in the United States. Two months later The Rolling Stones release their debut album.

Nelson Mandela is sentenced to life imprisonment in South Africa, convicted of the crime of inciting workers to strike.

In the wake of the Tonkin Gulf incident, in which U.S. destroyers are allegedly fired on by North Vietnamese patrol boats, President Lyndon Johnson signs the Gulf of Tonkin Resolution. Under the terms of this resolution, the U.S. will assist any south Asian nation that is threatened by Communist aggression.

1965
Canada unfurls its new red-and-white Maple Leaf flag.

The first U.S. combat troops arrive in South Vietnam.

1966
Beatle John Lennon states, "We're more popular than Jesus now," thereby triggering a huge controversy in the United States.

Davies and His Times

1967
Davies is commissioned to work on two projects for Canada's centennial celebrations. Neither comes to anything.

His *Marchbanks' Almanack* is published.

He and Brenda start work on their retirement home, Windhover, in the Caledon area. It will be completed in 1971.

Rupert Davies dies, March 11. Because he has already divided ownership of the *Peterborough Examiner* among his sons, he leaves the remainder of his estate to his grandchildren. Davies can't help but feel passed over. He must also work very hard to empty his father's estate in Wales and dispose of it.

Vincent Massey dies, December 30.

1968
The *Peterborough Examiner* is sold for $3.1 million. Davies receives thirty per cent of this sum.

Davies starts working on his best-known novel, *Fifth Business.*

Canada and the World

1967
Canada celebrates its centennial. The Expo '67 World Fair opens in Montreal.

The Six-Day War erupts between Israel and a coalition of Arab countries.

Multiple race riots break out across the United States.

1968
The North Vietnamese launch their Tet Offensive against a variety of U.S. targets in South Vietnam. American sentiment turns against the war.

In April, James Earl Ray shoots and kills Martin Luther King, Jr. in

Davies and His Times	*Canada and the World*
	Memphis, Tennessee. Two months later, Sirhan Sirhan assassinates Democratic presidential candidate Robert Kennedy in Los Angeles.
	Republican Richard Nixon wins the U.S. presidential race.
	Liberal leader Pierre Elliot Trudeau becomes prime minister of Canada.
	In an attempt to trigger a "May Revolution," French students strike and riot in Paris and come close to causing the government to fall.
	The "Prague Spring" or political liberalization of Czechoslovakia ends when Warsaw Pact troops invade the country.
1969 Davies's youngest daughter, Rosamond, marries Dr. John Paul Cunnington.	**1969** The Official Languages Act is passed in Canada, guaranteeing that English and French are the nation's official languages for the purposes of Parliament and government.
	Neil Armstrong is the first human to walk on the moon as part of NASA's Apollo 11 mission.
	The Woodstock Festival in upstate New York is attended by some 400,000 concertgoers.

Davies and His Times

1970
Davies's *Stephen Leacock* is published, but he is ashamed of its poor editing job.

Fifth Business appears. It receives glowing reviews, in Canada and elsewhere. Davies is now an internationally recognized author. He immediately sets to work on a sequel.

1972
The Manticore appears. It too receives very positive reviews. Davies wins the Governor General's Award for the book.

Davies becomes a Companion of the Order of Canada, in recognition of his outstanding lifetime achievements and dedication to Canadian culture.

Canada and the World

1970
The *Front de Libération du Québec* (FLQ) kidnaps British trade commissioner James Cross, beginning Canada's October Crisis. Five days later the FLQ kidnaps Quebec labour minister Pierre Laporte. Prime Minister Trudeau invokes the War Measures Act. Laporte is subsequently murdered.

1971
Canada is the first country to make multiculturalism official government policy.

1972
U.S. president Richard Nixon visits Communist China and holds extensive talks with Mao Zedong.

Police arrest five men at the Watergate Complex in Washington D.C. on charges of breaking and entering the Democratic National Committee headquarters. This crime will lead to the eventual resignation of U.S. president Richard Nixon.

Canada defeats Russia in hockey's Canada-Russia Summit Series.

Palestinian terrorists murder eleven Israeli athletes at the Summer Olympics in Munich.

Davies and His Times

Canada and the World

1973
After intense squabbling, Davies is forced to turn Massey College into a co-ed institution.

1973
In its decision Roe v. Wade, the U.S. Supreme Court overturns state bans on abortion.

The World Trade Center, with its famous Twin Towers, opens in New York City.

Egyptian and Syrian forces attack Israeli forces and trigger the Yom Kippur War.

1974
Quebec launches its Official Languages Act (Bill 22) which proclaims French as the official language of government in Quebec.

To avoid impeachment, U.S. president Richard Nixon becomes the first president to resign from office. He is pardoned by his successor, Gerald Ford.

1975
Davies's *World of Wonders* appears and concludes the Deptford Trilogy. The reviews are positive.

1975
The Vietnam War comes to an end when North Vietnamese forces capture Saigon.

Two assassination attempts are made on U.S. president Gerald Ford.

Davies and His Times

Canada and the World

1976

Davies starts taking notes for *The Rebel Angels*.

Film options are taken out on *Fifth Business* — Davies sells the rights for fifty thousand dollars — but no film materializes.

1976

The Parti Québecois forms the government in Quebec, under the leadership of Réné Lévesque.

The CN Tower opens in Toronto.

The Summer Olympics are held in Montreal.

Democrat Jimmy Carter wins the U.S. presidential race.

1977

Davies publishes *One Half of Robertson Davies*, a collection of essays on a variety of subjects.

1977

Bill 101 is passed in Québec. It stipulates the exclusive use of French by the provincial government, the courts, and businesses.

1978

Israeli prime minister Menachem Begin and Egyptian president Anwar Sadat sign the Camp David Accords.

1979

Davies starts writing *The Rebel Angels*.

Another collection of Davies's essays appears (compiled by Judith Skelton Grant): *The Enthusiasms of Robertson Davies*.

1979

The Shah of Iran leaves the country and the Ayatollah Khomeini returns from his exile in France. He initiates an Islamic Revolution. Nine months later extremists take American embassy staff members hostage. These tensions trigger a worldwide energy crisis.

Davies and His Times

Canada and the World

The Soviet Union invades Afghanistan.

1980
Quebeckers vote in a referendum on sovereignty-association with Canada. Sixty per cent vote "non." Prime Minister Trudeau presses forward with constitutional reform.

The United States boycotts the Summer Olympics that are being held in Moscow to protest the Soviet invasion of Afghanistan.

Republican Ronald Reagan wins the U.S. presidential race.

1981
The Rebel Angels appears. British author Anthony Burgess opines that Davies should receive the Nobel Prize for Literature.

1981
U.S. president Ronald Reagan sustains a non-lethal wound when he is shot by John Hinckley, Jr. in Washington, D.C.

Davies retires as master of Massey College.

The first recognized cases of AIDS appear in Los Angeles.

He writes a libretto for the children's opera *Dr. Canon's Cure*, the music for which is composed by Derek Holman.

1982
High Spirits is published — a collection of the ghost stories.

1982
Queen Elizabeth II signs an agreement that repatriates Canada's constitution and

Davies and His Times

Judith Skelton Grant approaches
Davies and proposes that she
write his biography. Davies
agrees. The book takes shape over
the next twelve years.

1985
What's Bred in the Bone appears
to great critical acclaim.

An omnibus of all three
Marchbanks books appears
under the title, *The Papers of
Samuel Marchbanks*.

1986
Davies is nominated for both
the Nobel Prize for Literature
and the Booker Prize, the most
coveted award for literature in
the English-speaking world. He
loses out to Wole Soyinka and
Kingsley Amis, respectively.

1988
The Lyre of Orpheus appears,
the final volume in the Cornish
Trilogy. By this stage, Davies has
sold hundreds of thousands of
copies of his books.

Canada and the World

grants Canada full political
independence from Britain.

Argentina invades the Falkland
Islands and precipitates a war
with Britain.

1984
Conservative Brian Mulroney
becomes the prime minister of
Canada.

1986
The space shuttle *Challenger*
bursts into flames shortly after
takeoff. All seven crew members
are killed.

1988
Russian premier Mikhail
Gorbachev initiates *Perestroika*,
or "reforms" to the Soviet
Union's economic structure.

Davies and His Times	*Canada and the World*
	Republican George H.W. Bush wins the U.S. presidential race.

1989
Chinese labour activists and students initiate protests in Beijing's Tiananmen Square. The military responds with violence and kills some two to three thousand citizens.

East Germany opens checkpoints along the Berlin Wall and permits the free passage of citizens. Civilians set to work demolishing the wall. The Soviet Union's hold on its Eastern European satellite states quickly slackens.

1990
After serving twenty-seven years behind bars, Nelson Mandela is released from prison.

At the behest of Saddam Hussein, Iraqi forces invade Kuwait. The United Nations passes Resolution 678, authorizing military force if Iraq fails to withdraw from Kuwait.

The Meech Lake Accord is defeated. It would have recognized Quebec as a distinct society and granted more influence to the provinces on federal governance.

Davies and His Times	*Canada and the World*
1991	**1991**
Murther and Walking Spirits appears. The reviews are lukewarm.	In the face of Iraqi non-compliance to withdraw its troops from Kuwait, Operation Desert Storm is initiated. Iraq launches Scud missiles against Israel.
	Boris Yeltsin is elected president of Russia. The Soviet Union is dissolved and the Commonwealth of Independent States is established in its place.
1992	**1992**
Assistant director Elliott Hayes adapts Davies's *World of Wonders* for the stage at Stratford. The success of this play stirs U.S. interest in rendering one of his novels into a movie.	Canadian provincial premiers put forward the Charlottetown Accord as a substitute for and improvement upon the failed Meech Lake Accord. It is defeated in a national referendum.
	Democrat Bill Clinton wins the U.S. presidential race.
1993	**1993**
While writing a screenplay for *A Mixture of Frailties* in Hollywood, Elliott Hayes is killed by a drunk driver. The project is never completed.	A truck bomb is detonated in the underground parking lot of the World Trade Center, killing six people. Muslim terrorists claim responsibility.
	Liberal leader Jean Chretien becomes the prime minister of Canada.

Davies and His Times

1994
The Cunning Man appears, the last of Davies's finished novels. It too proves disappointing in the critics' eyes.

Despite severe setbacks with his health, Davies starts taking notes for yet another novel.

Judith Skelton Grant's *Robertson Davies: Man of Myth* finally comes into print after twelve long years of research. Davies's response is ambivalent.

1995
In mid-November, Davies suffers a severe stroke. His ability to speak and write is affected. On December 2 he suffers a second, fatal stroke.

His funeral is conducted on December 5 at Trinity College. Obituaries appear in a vast array of international papers.

Canada and the World

1994
The North American Free Trade Agreement (NAFTA) takes effect.

Mass killings begin of Rwanda's Tutsi population by the majority Hutus. The death toll will be anywhere from 800,000 to one million people.

1995
Premier of Quebec Jacques Parizeau holds another referendum on Quebec independence. The pro-separatist faction is defeated by the narrowest of margins.

Israeli prime minister Yitzhak Rabin is assassinated by an Israeli extremist.

Bibliography

WORKS BY ROBERTSON DAVIES
(in order of publication)

Shakespeare's Boy Actors. London: Dent and Dutton, 1939.
Shakespeare for Young Players. Toronto: Clarke, Irwin & Co., 1942.
The Diary of Samuel Marchbanks. Toronto: Clarke, Irwin & Co., 1947.
The Table Talk of Samuel Marchbanks. Toronto: Clarke, Irwin & Co., 1949.
Fortune, My Foe. Toronto: Clarke, Irwin & Co., 1949.
Eros at Breakfast and Other Plays. Toronto: Clarke, Irwin & Co., 1949.
At My Heart's Core. Toronto: Clarke, Irwin & Co., 1950.
Tempest-Tost. Toronto: Clarke, Irwin & Co., 1951.
A Masque of Aesop. Toronto: Clarke, Irwin & Co., 1952.
Leaven of Malice. Toronto: Clarke, Irwin & Co., 1954.
A Jig for a Gypsy. Toronto: Clarke, Irwin and Co., 1954.
A Mixture of Frailties. Toronto: Macmillan, 1958.
A Voice from the Attic. New York: Alfred Knopf, 1960.
A Masque of Mr. Punch. Toronto: Oxford University Press, 1963.
Samuel Marchbanks' Almanack. Toronto: McClelland and Stewart, 1967.
Fifth Business. Toronto: Macmillan, 1970.
Stephen Leacock. Toronto: McClelland and Stewart, 1970.
The Manticore. Toronto: Macmillan, 1972.
Hunting Stuart and Other Plays. Toronto: New Press, 1972.
World of Wonders. Toronto: Macmillan, 1975.
One Half of Robertson Davies. Toronto: Macmillan, 1977.
The Enthusiasms of Robertson Davies, McClelland and Stewart, 1979.

The Rebel Angels. Toronto: Macmillan, 1981.
High Spirits. Toronto: Penguin, 1982.
What's Bred in the Bone. Toronto: Macmillan, 1985.
The Papers of Samuel Marchbanks. Toronto: Macmillan, 1985.
The Lyre of Orpheus. Toronto: Macmillan, 1988.
Murther and Walking Spirits. Toronto: McClelland and Stewart, 1991.
The Cunning Man. Toronto: McClelland and Stewart, 1994.
The Merry Heart. Toronto: McClelland and Stewart, 1996.
Happy Alchemy. Toronto: McClelland and Stewart, 1997.

SECONDARY WORKS CONSULTED

BUITENHUIS-CAMERON, Elspeth. *Robertson Davies.* Toronto: Forum House, 1972.

CAMERON, Elspeth. *Robertson Davies: An Appreciation.* Toronto: Broadview Press, 1991.

GRANT, Judith Skelton. *Robertson Davies: Man of Myth.* Toronto: Viking Penguin, 1994.

LA BOSSIERE, Camille. *Robertson Davies: A Mingling of Contrarities.* Ottawa: University of Ottawa Press, 2001.

MILLS, John. *Robertson Davies and His Works.* Toronto: ECW Press, 1984.

MORLEY, Patricia. *Robertson Davies.* Toronto: Gage Educational, 1977.

PETERMAN, Michael. *Robertson Davies.* Boston: Twayne Publishers, 1986.

ROSS, Val. *Robertson Davies: A Portrait in Mosaic.* Toronto: McClelland and Stewart, 2008.

Index

Fictional characters are listed alphabetically by their first names.

Marquis Book Printing Inc.

Québec, Canada
2009